ACTIVITIES
for
PARENT GROUPS

ACTIVITIES

— *for* —

PARENT GROUPS

*Structured Developmental Activities
for Parent Groups*

GARY B. WILSON

DELIVERING THE BEST RESOURCES TO EDUCATORS

**HUMANICS™
LEARNING**

HUMANICS™
LEARNING

PRINTED IN THE UNITED STATES IN AMERICA

Library of Congress Preassigned Catalog Card Number: 98-85985

ISBN 0-89334-165-7

10 9 8 7 6 5 4 3

Contents

CHAPTER 4: BUILDING AN EFFECTIVE GROUP   51

CHAPTER 5: GROUP PLANNING AND ORGANIZATION   66

CHAPTER 6: WORKING TOWARDS PROGRAM DEVELOPMENT 94

CHAPTER 7: EVALUATING THE TRAINING 110

GLOSSARY 117

SUGGESTED RESOURCE MATERIALS 119

READER EVALUATION FORM 120

Introduction

In every child development center or school, parents and staff share one common goal: to provide a quality educational program for the children. The parents entrust their most valuable possessions—their children—to these programs; many staff members invest more time in the child development center than anywhere else on a typical work day. The purpose of this book is to help groups of parents and teachers work together effectively to provide the type of program that best meets the needs of the children. It also delineates methods for implementing such a program on a day-to-day basis.

In *Activities for Parent Groups: Structured Developmental Activities for Parent Groups,* the author draws together a series of training exercises developed during his years of work with adults in educational settings. The introductory section presents the theories of parent involvement and adult education from which the training exercises were derived. In order to establish a base of common understanding between the author and the reader, these theories are related to the role of the teacher (i.e., trainer) in facilitating parent involvement in the child development program.

Recent studies of adult learning habits have refuted the commonly held notion that learning capacity decreases with age. These studies of adult perception, modes of behavior, and motivation indicate that the ways adults learn are significantly different from the ways children learn:

1. Adults learn only those skills or information they feel a need to learn.
2. Adults learn by doing (experience).
3. Adults learn by solving realistic problems.
4. Adults learn best in informal, interactive environments.
5. Adults learn best when a variety of training methods is employed.
6. Adults learn best by having input in the teaching methods.
7. Adults learn best in peer settings.

The exercises in this workbook incorporate all of the above principles. First, the exercises deal with common concerns facing parent involvement programs. They provide information that parents and teachers need to know to form *effective* parent groups.

Second, the exercises are *experiential.* Rather than presenting lectures for a trainer to regurgitate to the trainees, this manual offers various "experiences" through exercises which allow adults to "learn by doing."

Third, the exercises are structured around situations which are familiar to adults involved in educational programs. They present the parents and staff with *realistic,* rather than abstract, problems to be solved.

Fourth, the exercises are designed to create an *informal* setting to maximize adult learning. Several of them deal specifically with techniques for achieving a relaxed learning environment.

Finally, the exercises are designed to meet *individualized* needs. Using the diagnostic instruments found in the book, trainees learn to define their particular training needs and choose the focus of the exercises accordingly.

These exercises have been selected with a variety of techniques in mind. Each group chooses and adapts the exercises for its specific needs. Only those activities that are *relevant* to a group should be used.

Chapter 1
Overview

HOW TO USE THIS BOOK

To be effective, the trainer must be thoroughly familiar with the group being trained and its objectives in order to select training experiences that are appropriate for this group. The trainer must plan each lesson carefully but be flexible enough to adjust the sessions to meet unexpected changes in needs and objectives.

This book is not designed for use as a course curriculum in which a group begins at page one and continues to the end. Obviously, each program has unique training needs, and since various exercises presented in this book use different techniques to achieve the same purpose, it is not necessary to use them all. Instead, you will want to select the exercises appropriate to the specific needs of your group.

Most of the training exercises can be found in the following five chapters:

Chapter 2: Assessing the Situation is designed to assist the trainer in measuring staff members' perceptions about parent involvement and determining training needs.

Chapter 3: Coming Together is meant to help members become acquainted with one another and form a relaxed, informal group.

Chapter 4: Building an Effective Group will assist members in sharing knowledge and ideas with one another. Also in this chapter are exercises which can help a group determine interests and activities to be explored further.

Chapter 5: Group Planning and Organization will teach groups to work together effectively, to accept differing opinions, and to develop leadership skills useful in group interaction.

Chapter 6: Working Towards Program Development provides practical training experiences in the major policy and decision-making tasks of any child care center or school and is especially well suited for programs whose guidelines allow for extensive parent involvement.

Chapter 7: Evaluating the Training provides forms and suggestions for evaluating training sessions and improving training skills.

FOUR GENERAL STEPS IN TRAINING

Step 1: Preliminary survey of the situation.

This involves visits to the center/school and to the community which the program serves. Observations of the program's activities and conversations with staff and parents regarding their respective roles will help determine what needs to be accomplished. The survey will also give the trainer a sense of the "climate," or atmosphere, of the center/school, as well as an understanding of how the staff feels about its training needs. This is an important first step in preparing for formal meetings with the parents and staff.

The *Staff Assessment of Parent Involvement* exercise is meant to help the trainer measure staff members' perceptions of parent involvement. It should be used to supplement the trainer's own observations from conversations and meetings with staff, parents, and other persons in the community.

Step 2: Identification of training needs.

This step is essential in designing the training program and should include input from parents and staff. The trainer should assist the group in determining its training goals to ensure a training program which the members can call their own.

Since a major training objective is to assist the group in making its own decisions, the planning process provides a good place to start. The trainer should draw out ideas, observations and suggestions from the group, rather than feed information to a passive group. The group members also need to understand the purpose of the diagnostic instruments and how the data will be used.

The exercise, *Identifying Training Needs*, is designed to facilitate this process of diagnosis and assessment.

Step 3: Planning and implementation of training.

This step involves selecting the appropriate training exercises based on the identified needs and goals of the group. The trainer should utilize the data generated by the diagnostic exercises, keeping in mind the training techniques and adult education theories previously described. The exercises in **Chapters 3, 4, 5,** and **6** are provided for this purpose.

Step 4: Evaluation of training.

Instruments for training evaluation should serve two purposes:

1. To give the trainer the opportunity to evaluate the accomplishments of the training as well as his/her growth as a trainer.

2. To provide the participants with a forum to express their opinions about the training as well as their suggestions for future improvements.

PRINCIPLES OF PARENT INVOLVEMENT

The combination of input from both trainer and trainees will help in future planning sessions. Two sample forms included in **Chapter 7** are intended as guidelines for evaluation and can be easily tailored to fit individual training situations.

A. "Principle" is: 1. a rule of conduct.
2. a comprehensive and fundamental law, doctrine, or assumption.

B. "Assumption" is: 1. a fact or statement taken for granted.
2. the supposition that something is true.

The following statements include inherent assumptions. Try to determine the assumptions behind each:

"We won't need to spend much time explaining the guidelines to the parents at tomorrow night's meeting because I mailed a copy to each parent."

"Our meeting should go quite well tonight because I prepared an agenda and explained it to our chairperson. You know, she's the one who joined the group at the last meeting."

"As you know, our County Health Department has been uncooperative in regards to providing free dental screening to the center's children. Since the county commissioners said the decision is up to the Health Department and the funds are available, I have no doubt that if we take our work program down there and just explain the situation thoroughly, we could get the free screening."

"I am not going to plan a way home from the party tonight because lots of people will be there and somebody will give me a ride."

SOME PRINCIPLES OF PARENT INVOLVEMENT

Parents do care about their children. They will participate when they believe they are helping their children and are learning ways to become better parents.

Parents do care about their child care centers and schools and want these programs to continue. Parents will participate if they believe that, by doing so, they will make a difference. Just telling them that they make a difference does not cause them to believe—they must feel it.

Parents are adults. They do not like to sit in meetings if they feel useless, helpless, uncomfortable, or patronized. They must see the objectives of the program as meaningful and their roles as significant.

Exercise 1 is designed to help groups identify additional principles of parent involvement.

Exercise 1
PRINCIPLES OF PARENT INVOLVEMENT

Purpose: To define the goals of parent involvement and identify realistic ways to achieve these goals.

Setting: A room to accommodate a fully representative meeting of the staff and parents.

Time: Approximately two hours.

Materials: Newsprint (or large paper taped to the wall, on an easel, etc.), markers, masking tape, pencils, and a copy of *Worksheet 1: Principles of Parent Participation* for each person.

INSTRUCTIONS

1. Distribute a copy of *Worksheet 1* to each person. Divide the participants into small groups (five or less), and instruct each group to "brainstorm" a list of principles of parent participation. **[60 minutes]**

2. Call the groups together and have a representative from each write his/her group's list on newsprint in front of the room. Lead the group through a compare/contrast session to narrow the list down to meet the program's needs. **[30 minutes]**

3. Discuss which principles are absolutely essential and which are not as important and why. Talk about realistic ways to achieve these principles. **[30 minutes]**

Worksheet 1
PRINCIPLES OF PARENT PARTICIPATION

INSTRUCTIONS

List those principles you feel are necessary for **effective parent participation**. Use examples from your own experiences as much as possible, keeping the program's goals in mind.

1. ....

....

....

....

2. ....

....

....

....

3. ....

....

....

....

4. ....

....

....

....

5. ....

....

....

....

THE ROLE OF THE CHILD DEVELOPMENT CENTER OR SCHOOL

Every school or child development program has the potential to be a positive influence. This is possible when these programs maximize their resources to impact not only the children in the programs but also the community in which they are located. Parent involvement in the creation and direction of educational programs is essential for the following reasons:

Awareness of the Child's Environment.

For a program to provide a maximum learning experience for its children, the teaching staff should have the greatest possible awareness of each child's environment, including his or her educational experiences outside the classroom.

A child's education neither begins nor ends with the hours he or she spends in a child development center or school. Because a child's mind is constantly alert to new stimuli, every aspect of his or her life is an educational experience. Keeping this in mind will help teachers and staff to design activities that can be integrated into a child's culture and life experience. Otherwise, these activities may be perceived as different or "foreign", and the child will learn to see them as irrelevant to other aspects of his or her life. Since parents are vital sources of information about the child's home life, teachers and staff should maintain open communications with them. It is important that parents become aware of the goals, objectives, and activities of the program in order to reinforce the child's educational experience in the home setting. In this way, the time that the child spends in the center or school can become a more integrated and meaningful part of each day.

Since the most influential people in a child's life are his or her parents, parent reinforcement of the educational program will positively impact the child's capacity for learning. If a child senses that the parents are not involved in the program, his or her opportunity to experience an integrated education, which links the educational facility with the home, will decrease. In such cases, he or she may be forced to choose between the behavioral demands of parent and teacher, which may or may not be consistent. When a child knows that his or her parents are actively involved with the school or center, the potential for such conflicts is reduced.

Knowledge of Program.

The strength of a child development program is directly proportional to the degree of positive interaction between parents and educators. Parents have unique and important knowledge about their own children, which can be invaluable to the staff. This knowledge must be available to and utilized by the child development program if the various aspects of the child's needs are to be met. Conversely, staff members have knowledge of the program and its children, which needs to be shared with parents. When parents and staff work together, the planning and implementation of the program will involve the people who are most concerned with the success of the program.

Meaningful Assessment.

Active parent involvement also provides the staff with an opportunity to receive ongoing assessment of their efforts. If staff and parents communicate regularly, through both "formal" meetings and "informal" conversations, their relationship will be open and receptive. If parents know that their input is being heard and implemented, it will be much easier for the staff to obtain useful feedback on their efforts. This, in turn, will make the program more responsive to the needs of the children.

Support of Community.

If a child development program is to be successful, it must have the support of the surrounding community. Parents feel that the child development center or school is "theirs" if they are actively involved in planning its program and determining its direction. If this level of involvement is achieved, the child development program will be successfully integrated into the life of the community. The involvement and integrated activity may act as a catalyst for other community activities, fostering grassroots participation and commitment.

If, on the other hand, parents are not actively involved in the program and the policy making process, it is more likely that they will see the school or child development center as belonging to the Board of Education, the government, or the grantee agency or staff rather than to themselves. As a result, the child development program will be seen less as an undertaking by the community and more as an institution run by outside administrators. This may result in a corresponding lack of community support and may foster alienation from other institutions which exist to provide services to community residents.

To utilize available community resources successfully, one must understand how these institutions function, and how they can be influenced to best serve the needs of the community. In recent years, people have become more aware of the fact that residents of lower-income neighborhoods have little, if any, opportunity for meaningful involvement in the institutions that affect their lives.

By giving parents a voice in the policy and decision making processes in their children's education, the neighborhood school or child care center offers a good starting point for such a meaningful exchange. If parents gain confidence and experience through working with other parents and the staff for their children, they will be more inclined to participate in other local institutions, as well as to stay involved with their children throughout the course of their education.

EARLY CHILDHOOD DEVELOPMENT AND EDUCATION

Skills acquired early in a child's educational experience will prove valuable as the child moves through the educational system. In many communities, both public and private educational programs have been instrumental in introducing valuable support services as part of the educational process. These include the use of small classes with a low pupil-teacher ratio; the use of para-professional, community-wise teacher aides; the meaningful involvement of parents in their children's development and education; extensive medical and dental services; and increased attention to the special needs of each child. These features are already becoming commonplace in many public school systems.

If, as a part of the pre-school experience, parents play a major role in the planning, design, and execution of these support services, they will have a working knowledge of the benefits these programs yield and the resources required to provide the best educational experience possible for their children. As a result, the parents' ability to develop and expand such support services within the community will increase.

MAJOR KINDS OF PARENT PARTICIPATION

Active parents can do any or all of the following to get more involved in their children's educational program:

1. **Provide suggestions about the nature and operation of the program.**

    - Assist in development and operation of appropriate components of the program as delineated by teachers.
    - Work closely with staff to implement special activities, such as presentations for career day.
    - Plan, conduct, and participate in informal programs and activities for parents and staff.
    - Participate in the recruiting and screening of school or child care center employees under the supervision of staff.

2. **Participate as volunteer or observer.**

    - Visit the school or care center to observe the childrens' social interactions.
    - Volunteer to work with the children, help the staff prepare materials, and become involved in planning sessions for daily activities.
    - Assist in planning and making arrangements for activities which take place away from the school or center, such as field trips.

3. **Participate in parent-developed activities.**

    - Plan educational programs in areas which are of interest to the children and the parents.
    - Collaborate with other parents and staff to solve community problems which are of common concern, such as health, housing, education, and welfare.
    - Sponsor activities and programs which will benefit other families or child development programs.

4. **Work with children in the home along with the staff of the child development center or school.**

    - Parents should encourage home visits by staff members as an essential part of the overall educational program.
    - Parents can use staff home visits to exchange ideas on ways to extend the child's learning experiences into the home as well as make suggestions for program activities.

NOTES TO THE PARENT INVOLVEMENT TRAINER

This book is designed for use in a child development program by the person responsible for the staff training and the development of parent involvement. As the trainer, you might be a staff development coordinator, a parent involvement specialist, or a social services coordinator. You might also be a parent volunteer, a teacher, or a social worker who has been assigned this important responsibility. Whatever your background, prior training experiences may be helpful, but are not necessary to use this workbook. However, if you feel that you are particularly lacking in training experience, you might find the resources listed in the **Suggested Resource Materials** section helpful.

The exercises are designed to help parent groups become more independent and responsible. The trainer's task is to help groups achieve these objectives by stimulating effective and creative thinking in their trainees. The trainer is not a "teacher" in the traditional sense. His or her major objective of the training is not to impart new knowledge, but to help the trainees become aware of, utilize, and share the knowledge they already possess.

Our experience has shown us that the best way to begin developing an effective group of parents and staff is to create a relaxed climate which encourages openness. All members of the group should help the others feel important and encourage everyone to contribute ideas and suggestions. If all members feel free to share information and ideas, they will be able to work together to determine the goals of the program, suggest curriculum guidelines, and help in the decision making.

The trainer's attitude and manner will set the tone for the group climate. If you are relaxed, informal and friendly, the participants will most likely follow your example. Unless a specific exercise calls for a different arrangement, you should place the chairs in a circle or around a table so that participants can make eye contact. If available, light refreshments may help to make the meeting more informal and relaxed. It is also the trainer's responsibility to make sure that everyone has the opportunity to participate.

Because of the unique nature of adult education, a trainer should keep lectures and demonstrations to a minimum. You should try to ask questions, encourage an open exchange of ideas, listen creatively, draw out the participants' best thinking, and help them work cooperatively by minimizing or resolving conflicts.

Adults learn best by experience, and the trainer of parent groups is certainly no exception. The exercises in this book are designed to teach the participants as well as the trainer through experiences. They come with detailed information on the purpose, length of time and materials required; hints on training techniques; and clear instructions to the participants. Remember, prior training is not necessary, and it is only natural for you to initially feel somewhat confused and apprehensive.

Adult training, like any other specialized field, has developed its own set of terminology which may be confusing to the inexperienced trainer. To familiarize you with the training "lingo," we have included a glossary of terms which are frequently used in adult training. The definitions are cross-referenced as much as possible to the specific exercises that use these concepts.

Finally, an essential part of becoming an effective trainer is a continual process of self-evaluation. A careful assessment of accomplishments and new goals after each session is a valuable source of information in determining areas for further improvement in your training style. In addition, input from the participants can be helpful in your process of self-evaluation and should be solicited regularly. In **Chapter 7** of this book, we have presented a self-evaluation form for the trainer to complete after each session, as well as a session evaluation form for the participants.

Chapter 2
Assessing the Situation

The purpose of this chapter is to assist the trainer in measuring staff members' perceptions of parent involvement and in determining the training needs of the program.

The first step includes compiling and evaluating the data from the exercises in this section in order to determine the training needs of the group. The next step, designing and implementing the training program, is detailed in **Chapters 3, 4, 5,** and **6.**

Exercise 2
STAFF ASSESSMENT OF PARENT INVOLVEMENT

Purpose: To help the staff understand their present level of achievement and to help the staff identify training needs and goals in working with parents.

Setting: A room to accommodate a fully representative meeting of the staff with participants seated around a table.

Time: Approximately two hours.

Materials: Newsprint (or large paper taped to the wall or on an easel, etc.), markers, masking tape, pencils, and *Worksheet 2: Staff Assessment of Parent Involvement* for each participant.

INSTRUCTIONS

1. Begin by discussing the existing parent involvement in the program, focusing on the following points: [**30 minutes**]
   * *How was the parent group originally brought together?*
   * *How often has it met since it was formed?*
   * *What has it accomplished thus far?*
   * *What role has the staff played in involving and organizing parents?*
   * *If there is no parent group, what should be the first steps in starting one?*

2. After the discussion, distribute *Worksheet 2: Staff Assessment of Parent Involvement*, to be completed by each individual. [**15 minutes**]

3. Collect, shuffle, and redistribute the worksheets making sure no one receives his or her own paper. Everyone should read the responses and share the results in a discussion. [**45 minutes**]

4. Finally, lead the staff in an evaluation of the training skills needed by parent groups and the staff. [**30 minutes**]

Notes to the Trainer: This exercise is designed to encourage you and your participants to think ahead toward parent involvement training needs. Remember, the discussion is the focus of this exercise and the worksheet is a supplemental tool. In order to encourage openness, emphasize that there are no "right" or "wrong" answers to the questions. You may also use this same exercise later in the training program to determine changes in the participants' thinking and to assess progress in the training program.

16

Worksheet 2
STAFF ASSESSMENT OF PARENT INVOLVEMENT

INSTRUCTIONS

Answer the following questions as thoroughly and honestly as possible. Remember: there are no "right" or "wrong" answers to these questions. This worksheet will be used as the basis for a group discussion of parent involvement in your child development program. It is not necessary to put your name on this paper.

1. About parent groups:

    a. Does your program have a parent group?   YES ☐   NO ☐

    b. If not, do you wish to start one?   YES ☐   NO ☐

Why? _____

_____

2. About parents:

    a. What do they like about your present program?

_____

    b. What do they dislike about your present program?

_____

    c. What do they expect the present program to do for their children?

_____

    d. To what extent are these expectations being met by your present program?

_____

    e. How do they perceive their relationship to your program?

_____

    f. Are they involved in other community activities? Which ones?

_____

(continued)

(continued from page 17)

g. What kind of communication do they have with their children about your child care center or school?

....

h. What kind of communication do they have with you, the staff, about the child care center or school?

....

3. List any ideas contributed by individual parents or the parent group to the program:

....

....

4. List the most important goals you would like to see the parent group accomplish:

....

....

5. Responsibilities of the parents:

a. In your opinion, what types of responsibilities are the parents willing to accept?

....

....

b. In which of these areas would you like the parents to become more active?

❏ Volunteering time in the classroom

❏ Helping with painting, building and decorating

❏ Raising money for extra-curricular activities

❏ Deciding on equipment purchases

❏ Deciding on curriculum, materials and teaching approaches

❏ Researching and taking action on problems in the educational system

❏ Defining the perceived needs of the parent group

Other: ....

....

Exercise 3
IDENTIFYING TRAINING NEEDS

Purpose: To enable staff and parents to identify the type of help they need in their work with the school or child development program, and to enable staff and parents to become active participants by setting their own training goals.

Setting: A meeting of staff and parents in a room large enough to permit division into several groups of three or four, with minimal distraction.

Time: Approximately one hour.

Materials: Pencils, paper, markers, masking tape, and newsprint.

INSTRUCTIONS

1. Divide the participants into two groups: staff and parents. Subdivide the members of each group into sub-groups of three. You may ask one-third of the members to select the two people they know best or the two people they know least, etc.

2. Give each sub-group pencils and paper and instruct them to collaborate in listing their concerns about the following three categories:

   ✎   **The Children.** What they see the children's needs to be and how they themselves can become better equipped to deal with those needs.

   ✎   **Themselves as Parents or Staff.** Personal needs or perceived needs of the group.

   ✎   **The Other Group.** Define their relationship with the other group and determine some communication needs.

3. The sub-groups may also rank the items in each of these three categories in the order of importance. It may be more difficult to reach consensus in this task than in the first one. If time is a factor, the rank ordering may be limited to the division of major and minor concerns. [**20 minutes**]

(continued)

(continued from page 19)

4. After the groups have listed and ranked the three categories, the sub-groups should come together into two groups (staff and parents) to examine and compare their lists. A composite list should be made up on a sheet of newsprint. This list may also be ranked in order of importance. **[20 minutes]**

5. The two groups should then come together so that the trainer may lead a discussion focusing on:

1. Items that may have been listed by both parents and staff (needs which they agree upon).
2. Suggestions for courses of action to meet training needs.
3. How the members feel about one another.
[20 minutes]

Notes to the Trainer: The trainer might want to have a blank sheet of newsprint on the wall next to the composite list so that the suggested solutions can be recorded next to each problem. You should not hesitate to make suggestions based on personal experience, especially if the discussion is dragging, but do not dominate the discussion if it seems to be going at a healthy pace.

Exercise 4
ASSESSMENT OF WORK GROUP

Purpose: To assess the needs of the group and to set priorities.

Setting: A room large enough to accommodate several small groups.

Time: Approximately 30 minutes.

Materials: Markers, newsprint, and copies of *Worksheet 3: Summary of Child and Family Needs*.

INSTRUCTIONS

1. Divide everyone into small groups of three or four. Distribute a copy of *Worksheet 3* for each group to complete.

2. Once the worksheets are filled out, gather the groups together and have a representative from each write his or her group list on the newsprint.

3. Lead a discussion with everyone to compile and prioritize a common list. This activity is intended to document the needs and action plans of the group to be used in program development.

Worksheet 3
SUMMARY OF CHILD AND FAMILY NEEDS

INSTRUCTIONS

In groups of three or four, complete the following lists. As a group, prioritize the items on each list (low priority=L, high priority=H) and answer questions five and six. Choose a representative to present your group's answers to all the participants.

Priority Ranking
L=Low   H=High

1. List the needs of children and families:

....

....

....

....

2. List any services available to meet these needs:

....

....

....

....

3. List any community services available to meet these needs:

....

....

....

....

4. List possible changes that need to occur within the child development program or school to address these needs:

....

....

....

....

22   (continued)

(continued from page 22)

5. Explain your group's priority ranking:

....

....

....

....

6. How could you integrate certain components so that they do not conflict?

....

....

....

....

Notes

....

....

....

....

....

....

....

....

....

....

....

Chapter 3
Coming Together

The purpose of this chapter is to assist the staff and the parent group in creating a relaxed atmosphere for maximum comfort and productivity.

The following four chapters are sequential. A group will usually need to complete one or more of the exercises in **Chapter 3** before it is ready to learn the techniques presented in **Chapters 4, 5,** and **6.**

As a group proceeds through this chapter, the data obtained from the diagnostic instruments in **Chapter 2** should help in the selection of appropriate exercises. For example, if the parents and staff indicated a need to get to know each other better, *Exercise 9: Parent/Staff Perceptions* should be chosen. If the group expressed concerns regarding a domineering leadership, *Exercise 10: Role-Play—Bringing New People into an Established Group* may be appropriate.

Exercise 5
EXPLORING WHO I AM

> **Purpose:** To enable each parent or staff member to focus on himself or herself as a person and have parents and staff to get to know each other better.
>
> **Setting:** A room for any size group of parents and staff.
>
> **Time:** Approximately one hour.
>
> **Materials:** Pencils and *Worksheet 4: Exploring Who I Am,* for each participant.

INSTRUCTIONS

1. Ask the participants to go over this exercise individually, following the instructions on the handout sheet.

2. They should then select partners or form small groups of five or less and repeat the process, this time, sharing the information with each other.

3. If the participants feel comfortable enough, ask them to share their experiences with the larger group.

Worksheet 4
EXPLORING WHO I AM

INSTRUCTIONS

1. This is a tool to explore the question, "Who am I?" It's a tool for you, so disregard any part of it that does not fit or seem right for you. By using this tool you will find some of the many ways you can answer the question, "Who am I?" Sit quietly and write a description of yourself:

Describe your appearance:

HEIGHT: _____ ' _____ "

WEIGHT: _____ lbs

AGE: _____

HAIR COLOR: _____

EYE COLOR: _____

ETHNICITY: _____

Describe your past experiences:

What was your childhood like?

_____

_____

_____

Where have you lived?

_____

_____

_____

List the various roles you play (i.e., mother, friend, teacher):

_____

_____

_____

(continued)

(continued from page 26)

Describe your likes and dislikes:

_____

_____

_____

Describe your vision and goals for the next five years:

_____

_____

_____

Describe the most important relationships in your life:

_____

_____

_____

Exercise 6
SELF-KNOWLEDGE QUESTIONNAIRE

Purpose: To enable parents or teachers to become comfortable in small group settings.

Setting: A room large enough to accommodate eight to twelve members.

Time: Approximately 45 minutes.

Materials: Pencils, *Worksheet 5: Self-Knowledge Questionnaire*, and *Worksheet 6: Your Strengths* for each participant.

INSTRUCTIONS

1. Ask the participants to form small groups of three to six people.

2. Instruct them to answer both questionnaires and then share the results within their small groups.

Worksheet 5
SELF-KNOWLEDGE QUESTIONNAIRE

INSTRUCTIONS

Answer the following questions and share your answers with the others in your small group.

1. When I enter a new group, I feel:

2. When people meet me, their first impressions of me is:

3. When I'm in a new group, I feel most comfortable when:

4. When people remain silent, I feel:

5. When someone does all the talking, I:

6. I feel most productive when a leader:

(continued)

7. I feel annoyed when the leader:

_____

_____

8. I feel withdrawn when:

_____

_____

9. In a group, I am most afraid of:

_____

_____

10. When someone feels hurt, I:

_____

_____

11. I am hurt most easily when:

_____

_____

12. I feel loneliest in a group when:

_____

_____

13. Those who really know me think I am:

_____

_____

(continued)

(continued from page 30)

14. I trust those who:

_____

_____

15. I am saddest when:

_____

_____

16. I feel closest to others when:

_____

_____

17. People like me when I:

_____

_____

18. My greatest strengths are:

_____

_____

19. My favorite activity to do is:

_____

_____

Worksheet 6
YOUR STRENGTHS

An **"affirmation"** is: 1. the act of affirming or asserting something as true;
2. positive declaration.

INSTRUCTIONS

1. Based on your answers from the previous exercise, list all positive aspects of your character as personal affirmations.

2. Write down as many of your positive attributes as possible to complete the following sentence:

MY AFFIRMATIONS AS A PERSON
"I AM A ..."

1. _____

2. _____

3. _____

4. _____

5. _____

6. _____

7. _____

8. _____

9. _____

10. _____

Exercise 7
SCAVENGER HUNT

Purpose: To get to know each other.

Setting: A room to accommodate a large group of fifteen or more.

Time: Approximately 45 minutes.

Materials: Pencils and *Worksheet 7: Scavenger Hunt Questionnaire.*

INSTRUCTIONS

1. The object of the game is to find people who meet the criteria on *Worksheet 7: Scavenger Hunt Questionnaire.* Everyone should walk around the room and ask each other if they fit any of the descriptions.

Worksheet 7
SCAVENGER HUNT QUESTIONNAIRE

INSTRUCTIONS
Find a person who fits the following descriptions and write their name in the space provided.

1. Someone who has been to Disneyland:

2. Someone who has seen a U2 concert:

3. Someone who has piloted an airplane:

4. Someone who has never flown on an airplane:

5. Someone who voted for the current president:

6. Someone who has run for public office:

7. Someone who has quit smoking:

8. Someone who has been to Europe:

9. Someone who has been to Washington, D.C:

10. Someone who has made a quilt:

11. Someone who can swim:

12. Someone who dances at Powwows:

13. Someone who plays a musical instrument:

14. Someone who can make fried bread:

(continued)

(continued from page 34)

15. Someone who wears contact lenses:

16. Someone who has picked an orange from a tree:

17. Someone who has been at sea:

18. Someone who has won in Las Vegas:

19. Someone who has overhauled a car engine:

20. Someone who has gone to the National Rodeo finals:

21. Someone who can snow ski:

22. Someone who wears size 6 shoes:

23. Someone who has never been to a dentist:

24. Someone who has been to Canada:

25. Someone who has been to Mexico:

26. Someone who has won over $1,000 at bingo:

27. Someone who is bilingual:

28. Someone who wasn't born in the United States:

29. Someone who was in Head Start:

30. Someone who has lived in New York:

Exercise 8
YOU AND YOUR CHILD

Purpose: To enable parents to focus on their roles as parents.

Setting: Room for small groups.

Time: Approximately 30 minutes.

Materials: *Worksheet 8: You and Your Child Questionnaire.*

INSTRUCTIONS
1. Have participants form small groups to discuss each item on the questionnaire.

Worksheet 8
YOU AND YOUR CHILD QUESTIONNAIRE

INSTRUCTIONS

Answer the following questions as thoroughly and as honestly as possible.

1. What activities do you like to do with your child?

2. What are your hopes and plans for your child?

3. What activities does your child like to do?

4. What are you happiest doing with your child?

5. What are some of the problems you have living with your child?

6. What does your child do to make you happy?

Exercise 9
PARENT/STAFF PERCEPTIONS

Purpose: To provide an opportunity for parents and staff to examine their perceptions of each other and to reduce the "perception gap" between parents and staff.

Setting: A room to accommodate any size group of parents and staff.

Time: Approximately one hour.

Materials: Newsprint, markers (many colors), and masking tape.

INSTRUCTIONS

1. Divide the participants into two groups: staff and parents. Subdivide the members of each group into sub-groups of four or five.

2. Instruct each sub-group to draw two pictures on newsprint, one depicting how they perceive themselves (as parents or staff) and the other reflecting how they see the other group. [**30 minutes**]

3. Have the sub-groups hang their pictures up around the room and have a representative from each explain the pictures to everyone. Follow up with a general discussion on the contents of the pictures, led by the group representatives. [**30 minutes**]

Notes to the Trainer: Keep the focus of the discussion on the two groups' perceptions of each other and how to utilize this information to improve parent participation in the program.

During the final discussion, you might want to draw a composite picture, representing the input of both groups, on a sheet of newsprint as the discussion proceeds.

Exercise 10
ROLE-PLAY: BRINGING NEW PEOPLE INTO AN ESTABLISHED GROUP

Purpose: To help participants deal with situations, where others are dominating, by having them role-play various characters. Also, to assist parents and staff to increase parent involvement in the child care program's activities.

Setting: A meeting room for parents and staff, any size.

Time: Approximately one and a half hours.

Materials: Newsprint, markers, *Worksheet 9: Role-Play,* and video tape recording equipment (optional).

INSTRUCTIONS

1. Start with a brief explanation of the techniques and purpose of role- playing. Explain that the volunteer "actors" will be given parts to play, but no script, and that improvisation is intended to provide insight into the situation and to reflect the different views represented in the various roles. It will also help develop the skills needed to increase parent participation. [**10 minutes**]

2. Distribute *Worksheet 9: Role-Play* to the group members and allow them a few minutes to study the material. You should encourage the group to voice any questions about the situation to be role-played and the purpose of the exercise. [**10 minutes**]

3. Pick four volunteers to play the roles designated in *Worksheet 9*. Have the volunteers seat themselves at the front of the room. Allow ample time for the volunteers to review their roles and the instructions. Ask the audience not to laugh or comment while the role-play is taking place. If video recording equipment is available, record the role-play for reviewing purposes later. You should also pay close attention to the role-play so that you can stop it when it has ceased to be productive. Following the role-play, ask each volunteer to give his or her reactions to the exercise. [**70 minutes**]

Worksheet 9: ROLE-PLAY

INSTRUCTIONS

It is important to give the volunteers an opportunity to critique themselves before the audience gives their observations. You may lead the volunteers in a brief process evaluation, asking them whether they think they did well, whether they would change or improve their performances, and whether they gained any insight into the situation or the characters they were playing. When this process evaluation has been completed, you may then ask the audience to comment on the role-play as they observed it.

If the role-play exercise has been recorded, the tape may now be played so the volunteers can observe themselves. If time permits, you may want to repeat the role-play exercise with different players.

Following the completion of the role-play and the process evaluation, the trainer should reseat the players with the main group and lead a discussion of the content of the exercise. Some points to be covered might include:

1. How the situation applies to their child development program.

2. How the problems can be remedied.

Suggestions may be listed on three sheets of newsprint taped to the wall, so that the relationship of ideas is clearly visible.

Many people may be self-conscious about acting in front of an audience. A role-play exercise will only be successful if a group is relaxed and comfortable. The members of the group should at least be acquainted with one another before attempting the exercise and, under no circumstances, should anyone be pressured to participate. You might want to conduct one of the other exercises in this chapter as a "warm-up" before the role-play is attempted. You might also wish to consult the definition of role-playing in the Glossary for further information.

(continued)

(continued from page 40)

Purpose:

Parents are often hesitant to become involved in a program's activities because they feel the "same old group" of people are always running the show, and that their own participation will not make any difference. The following role-play exercise will examine this problem.

Plot:

The Parent Executive Committee is composed of parents whose children have been enrolled in the program for at least a year. This committee has controlled the parent group for two years. The principal of the school thinks that the present Parent Executive Committee members are dominating the parent meetings and are discouraging other parents from participating. The Parent Executive Committee, on the other hand, feels that the other parents lack the initiative to participate and if they themselves do not take control, nothing will get done.

The Scene:

Your child development program has been having difficulty getting parents to attend parent group meetings. Initially, many parents came to the meetings, but by the third meeting, attendance dropped off drastically. A meeting of the Parent Executive Committee has been called to discuss the problem of poor attendance at parent meetings.

The Participants:

School Principal: Mrs. Bold, a 38-year-old, married woman, has a reputation for "getting things done." She is experienced in working with adults as a Head Start teacher and as a representative for her school's teachers' union.

President of the Parent Executive Committee: Mrs. Loud, a 32-year-old mother of three, is a community social worker. She has been the president of the Parent Executive Committee for two years.

Vice-President of the Parent Executive Committee: Mr. Order, a 30-year-old father of three, has one child attending the school. He is a city maintenance worker who tends to be very critical. One of his main concerns is the school's inability to discipline the children.

Parent Executive Committee Member: Mrs. Golden, a 62-year-old grandmother, has a granddaughter that lives with her and attends the school. She has been an active member in both the community and the school system, and feels that the school can do no wrong.

Exercise 11
THE LEMON GAME—IDENTIFYING
INDIVIDUAL & COMMON INTERESTS

Purpose: To help participants distinguish between interests that are unique to them as parents and teachers, and common interests of the group.

Setting: A room for a group of ten to thirty parents and/or teachers to sit in a circle.

Time: Approximately one hour.

Materials: Newsprint, marker, one lemon for each participant, a large paper bag to hold the lemons, water, sugar, a pitcher, and paper cups or glasses.

INSTRUCTIONS

1. Give each participant a lemon. Allow five minutes for everyone to become familiar with his or her lemon: to study its particular characteristics (shape, coloring, scars, etc.); to try to think of a name for it; to imagine something of its "life history." Part of the time might be spent by touching the lemon with eyes closed. [**5 minutes**]

2. As creatively as possible, introduce your lemon to the group and let everyone else have a turn. The participants will probably be surprised to discover how simple and enjoyable this task is. After the introductions, put all the lemons in a paper bag and then dump them into a pile. [**20 minutes**]

3. Ask the participants to comment on the experience while you record their comments on newsprint. Make the analogy that both groups of lemons and groups of people contain individual, as well as common, features. In a group of parents and staff members, there will be individual interests, as well as common interests shared by all. Draw a chart on the newsprint and ask the group to list some of their individual and common interests. [**20 minutes**]

4. When the list is complete, the group should discuss ways in which the child

42   (continued)

(continued from page 42)

development program could be strengthened by building on the common interests of the group, and ways in which it might satisfy the individual interests of the members. [**15 minutes**]

Notes to the Trainer: To continue the exercise, make lemonade from the juice of the lemons, water, and sugar. While filling and distributing the glasses, make the analogy that the group is actually using resources drawn from individual contributions to achieve a common group goal. Participants can discuss other ways in which they can use resources available to them to achieve goals which are common to the group, such as improving and strengthening the child development program.

This exercise is enjoyable and can serve as an ice-breaker with new groups. The results of this game may also provide a basis for later training exercises in planning, setting goals, and understanding differences.

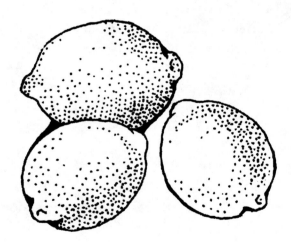

Exercise 12
SUCCESSFUL CHILDREN

Purpose: To help parents become aware of the group's perceptions of what constitutes successful children.

Setting: A room for any size group of parents.

Time: Approximately two hours.

Materials: Newsprint, magic markers, copies of *Worksheet 10: Characteristics of Successful Children*, and pencils for each participant.

INSTRUCTIONS

Explain the purpose of the exercise and discuss both positive and negative aspects of the characteristics listed. Make sure the group discusses ways to foster each characteristic in the children.

Worksheet 10
CHARACTERISTICS OF SUCCESSFUL CHILDREN

INSTRUCTIONS

The following are common characteristics of successful and well-adjusted children. You may also add to the list any traits you feel should have been included. Rank the characteristics according to your opinion of their importance, "1" being the most important, then "2" and so on. [**10 minutes**]

_____ A. Self-Confidence

_____ B. Assertiveness

_____ C. Popularity with Peers

_____ D. Spontaneity and Originality

_____ E. Ability to Complete Difficult Tasks

_____ F. High Self-Esteem

_____ G. Cooperation with Others

_____ H. Independence

_____ I. Self-Acceptance

_____ J. High Achievement in School

_____ K. Creativity

_____ L. Honesty and Openness

_____ M. Ability to Take Care of Self

_____ N. Acceptance of Others

_____ O. Ability to Follow Directions

_____ P. _____

_____ Q. _____

_____ R. _____

Exercise 13
COMMON ORGANIZATIONAL PROBLEMS

> **Purpose:** To familiarize parents and staff with the eight most common problems facing parent groups.
>
> **Setting:** A room for a small group.
>
> **Time:** Approximately 45 minutes.
>
> **Materials:** Copies of *Worksheet 11: Eight Common Organizational Problems.*

INSTRUCTIONS

1. Divide everyone into small groups of four or five. Have each group review the eight items on *Worksheet 11* and discuss each problem as it applies to the group.

2. Gather the groups together and have a representative from each share his/her group's thoughts with everyone.

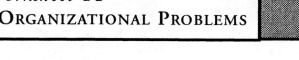

Worksheet 11
EIGHT COMMON ORGANIZATIONAL PROBLEMS

INSTRUCTIONS
Comment on how the following problems apply to your group. Please be as specific as possible.

Organizational Problems

1. Communication problems among organizational members.

2. Insufficient performance feedback.

3. Restrictive procedures (i.e. not enough time, one person monopolizing the discussion, etc.).

4. Overly frequent changes in organizational structure.

(continued)

47

(continued from page 47)

5. Management's resistance to change.

_____

_____

_____

_____

6. Disruptive rumors.

_____

_____

_____

_____

7. Political maneuvering.

_____

_____

_____

_____

8. Inter-group conflict.

_____

_____

_____

_____

Exercise 14
ADMINISTRATION OR POLICY FUNCTIONS

Purpose: To enable groups to understand the difference between a group's administrative and policy roles.

Setting: A room for small groups.

Time: Approximately 30 minutes.

Materials: None required.

INSTRUCTIONS

Participants will determine which statements on the accompanying handout deal with policy making and which deal with administrative duties.

Worksheet 12
ADMINISTRATION AND POLICY FUNCTIONS

INSTRUCTIONS

The statements listed below indicate either a Policy or Administrative function. Identify the Administrative function with an "A" and the Policy function with a "P."

____ 1. The program needs to establish criteria for enrollment.

____ 2. Parents need to be notified of their child's acceptance or rejection to the school or program.

____ 3. The bus breaks down and needs immediate repair.

____ 4. A child's immunization record needs to be updated before he returns to the school or center.

____ 5. An injured child at the center needs to be taken to the doctor.

____ 6. Qualifications for staff need to be determined.

____ 7. The program needs to determine the location of new center sites.

____ 8. Community Representatives appointed to serve on the Policy Council need to be approved.

____ 9. The Grant Application needs to be approved for the next fiscal year.

____ 10. An employee should be reprimanded for a violation of his or her job description.

____ 11. Criteria for bus drivers' performance needs to be established.

____ 12. Attendance on a daily basis needs to be reviewed.

____ 13. Lunch menus need to be reviewed and approved.

____ 14. Agendas for meetings need to be developed.

____ 15. Employee's performance needs to be evaluated.

____ 16. Sick child at the center needs attention.

Chapter 4
Building an Effective Group

The purpose of this chapter is to help parent groups become aware of commonalities among members which can be used to improve the child development program, and to determine various interests and activities which members may want to explore together.

As with **Chapter 3**, the trainer may want to refer back to the data generated by the diagnostic instruments in **Chapter 2**. This will help in the evaluation of the group's training needs in the area of inter-group communication and selection of exercises to meet those needs. For example, if the parents and staff have expressed dissatisfaction with the productivity of their meetings, *Exercise 20: Formal and Informal Meetings* may be a good exercise. If parent group members have indicated that they feel ill-at-ease in the presence of some or all of the staff, you might want to try one of the quick exercises in *Exercise 26* of **Chapter 5** to ease the feelings of tension, and so on.

Exercise 15
GUIDE FOR PRODUCTIVE MEETINGS

Purpose: To familiarize groups with the elements of a productive meeting.

Setting: A room for small groups.

Time: Approximately one hour.

Materials: *Worksheet 13: Elements of Productive Meetings.*

INSTRUCTIONS

First, divide everyone into small groups of four or five to discuss the items on *Worksheet 13*. Then, bring the groups together to discuss ways to improve meetings.

Worksheet 13
ELEMENTS OF PRODUCTIVE MEETINGS

INSTRUCTIONS

Using the following as a sample, develop your group's guidelines for a productive meeting.

1. Planning

    a. Establish objectives for meeting.

    b. Solicit group input for setting regular meeting time, place, procedures, etc.

    c. Secure facilities (convenient, free of distractions, comfortable, etc.).

2. Informing

    a. Establish procedure for notifying others.

    b. Schedule calendar (yearly, monthly, etc.).

    c. Notify participants of meeting time, location, and objectives.

    d. Distribute agenda before meeting.

    e. Describe responsibilities of participants.

3. Preparing

    a. Confirm attendance of participants.

    b. Complete any activities that require preparation prior to meeting (such as graphs, charts, handouts, and other materials and data).

    c. Assign management responsibilities to individuals (chair persons, committee leaders, etc.).

4. Proceeding

    a. Begin on time.

    b. Review agenda, prioritize items, schedule time.

    c. Follow agenda.

    d. Report from Component Coordinators, Committee Chair persons.

    e. Structure time loosely for open discussions or new business.

5. Recording

    a. Assign someone to record discussions and decisions; you might want to use a tape recorder.

    b. Review accomplishments before adjourning.

    c. Distribute copies of minutes to participants and other interested persons.

Exercise 16
TECHNIQUES FOR EFFECTIVE MEETING PARTICIPATION

Purpose: To give group members preliminary skills for effective meeting participation.

Setting: A room for a large group.

Time: Approximately one hour.

Materials: Copies of *Worksheet 14: Techniques for Effective Meetings*.

INSTRUCTIONS

Assign a specific role to each participant (Chairman, Secretary, Parent Representative, Staff Representative, Members, Treasurer, etc.). Simulate a formal decision-making meeting using *Worksheet 14: Techniques for Effective Meetings*.

Note to the Trainer: For more information about meeting procedures, consult *Roberts' Rules of Order*, from which these rules have been adapted.

INSTRUCTIONS

Use the following techniques in your simulated meeting.

If you want to...

1. Stop the meeting for a short time.

2. Set a time for the next meeting.

3. Focus the discussion on the main subject or point of the agenda.

4. Correct a mistake that is against the by-laws of the group.

5. Get more information on the business being discussed.

6. Question a chairperson's decision.

7. Have a discussion without being confined to the existing rules.

8. Stop a motion you have made.

9. Prevent discussion of a motion.

10. Have a motion put aside.

11. Bring up a motion that has been tabled.

   You say to the Chairman:

   I move we recess.

   I move we set the next meeting time.

   I call for the orders of the day.

   I rise to a point of order.

   I rise to a point of information.

   I appeal the decision of the chair.

   I move that we suspend the rules.

   I wish to withdraw the motion.

   I object to consideration of the motion.

   I move we table the motion.

   I move the motion be taken from the table.

(continued)

(continued from page 55)

Notes: Statements 4 to 9 are not debatable and can be made and voted on at any time except while any of the first 4 statements is being considered. Statements 4, 5, 7, and 9 need no second motion. Statements 7 and 9 require a vote of ⅔ to pass.

Motions 10 to 15 can be made when no other motions are being considered. All require a second motion. Motions 10 and 11 are not debatable.

Exercise 17
X-RAY OF THE PARENT/TEACHER

Purpose: To allow parents and staff to look at their own personal resources and evaluate ways to apply them effectively to the child development program.

Setting: A large carpeted room with chairs removed; a group of parents and staff, any size.

Time: Approximately one and a half hours.

Materials: Newsprint or any large pieces of paper, magic markers, masking tape, and copies of *Worksheet 15: X-Ray Guide*, for each participant.

INSTRUCTIONS

Have everyone pair up with someone he/she does not know very well. Ask the partners to share with each other any attributes they have to offer to improve the center or school program. [**10 minutes**]

Hand out *Worksheet 15: X-Ray Guide*, newsprint, and magic markers to each participant and instruct everyone to work on his/her own "X-Ray's". After they have finished, ask the partners to share the results with each other. [**55 minutes**]

Ask the participants to hang their "X-Rays" around the room with masking tape (names are optional). Then tell them to walk around the room to view each "X-Ray". After they are finished viewing, have everyone sit on the floor in a circle. Lead a discussion to come up with one "X-Ray" that is a composite of the entire group's resources. [**25 minutes**]

Worksheet 15
X-RAY GUIDE

INSTRUCTIONS

Lie down on your newsprint and have your partner outline your body with a marker. Fill in your silhouette with the following information:

1. **Head and Heart:** What I want and what I have to give as a parent or teacher.

2. **Torso:** Unresolved situations or problems.

3. **Left Hand:** Those skills that I need as a parent or teacher.

4. **Right Hand:** Those skills that I have to give as a parent or teacher.

5. **Right Leg:** My present role within the group.

6. **Left Leg:** My future role within the group.

Exercise 18
STAFF/PARENT RELATIONSHIP RATING SKILLS

Purpose: Assess the effectiveness of the staff in parent involvement and provide feedback in a positive setting.

Setting: Space for all the individuals to work alone.

Time: Approximately 45 minutes.

Materials: Copies of *Worksheet 16: Staff/Parent Relationship Rating Scale.*

INSTRUCTIONS

Hand out enough copies of *Worksheet 16: Staff/Parent Relationship Rating Scale* to each person so he/she can rate all the staff members (example: for 10 staff members you need to give each individual 10 worksheets). Explain that the purpose of this exercise is to offer constructive criticism.

Worksheet 16
STAFF/PARENT RELATIONSHIP RATING SCALE

INSTRUCTIONS

For each of the following, rate a staff member or parent. Put his/her name in the line provided and use one worksheet per staff member or parent. Leave blank if a question does not apply. You do not have to write your name on this sheet. (1—low, 7—high)

Name of Staff Member or Parent rated: ....

  1. Ability to give and take clear work instructions: 1 2 3 4 5 6 7

  2. Friendliness towards fellow staff members: 1 2 3 4 5 6 7

  3. Ability to work well with others (Team Work):   1 2 3 4 5 6 7

  4. Respect for and by other staff members: 1 2 3 4 5 6 7

  5. Ambitious: 1 2 3 4 5 6 7

  6. Ability to offer positive feedback other staff members: 1 2 3 4 5 6 7

  7. Pride in own work: 1 2 3 4 5 6 7

  8. Fairness in dealing with differences of opinion: 1 2 3 4 5 6 7

  9. Honesty in dealings with people: 1 2 3 4 5 6 7

10. Tendency to trust others: 1 2 3 4 5 6 7

11. Gossip about or criticism of others: 1 2 3 4 5 6 7

12. Presentable physical appearance (dress/hygiene):   1 2 3 4 5 6 7

13. Racial prejudice: 1 2 3 4 5 6 7

14. Ability to influence or inspire others: 1 2 3 4 5 6 7

15. Ability to control anger: 1 2 3 4 5 6 7

16. Knowledge of the program: 1 2 3 4 5 6 7

17. Supervision and leadership skills: 1 2 3 4 5 6 7

18. Creativity in work: 1 2 3 4 5 6 7

19. Contributes to the staff as a team member: 1 2 3 4 5 6 7

20. Signs of professional growth and development: 1 2 3 4 5 6 7

Exercise 19
HELPING OR BLOCKING COMMUNICATION

Purpose: To help participants recognize those elements that facilitate communication and those that block it. Also to enable participants to exchange their views on parent involvement.

Setting: Room for groups of six to eight people, staff and/or parents, in any combination.

Time: Approximately one hour.

Materials: Magic markers and newsprint.

INSTRUCTIONS

First have the participants brainstorm and discuss ideas on how to facilitate communication, drawing on their own experiences. Then have them list these ideas on newsprint, taped to the wall. **[20 minutes]**

Note to the Trainer: During this part of the exercise, participants should be instructed to make a mental note of the ways communication is being facilitated in the discussion itself.

Then, have the participants discuss ways communication is blocked, again drawing on personal experience. Ask them to list these on another sheet of newsprint, while keeping in mind any blocks to communication that are cropping up in the discussion. **[20 minutes]**

Afterwards, ask the participants to share feelings about ways to increase parent involvement. Before each person can speak, he/she must "earn the privilege" by summarizing what the previous speaker has said. **[20 minutes]**

Note to the Trainer: When time is called on the last portion of this exercise, the groups should be brought together for a general discussion, focusing on the following points:
1. Which factors were helping or blocking communication in the exercise?
2. Were the lists helpful in analyzing how discussions were flowing?
3. Did awareness of the process of communication result in a more meaningful discussion?

(continued)

(continued from page 61)

4. Does having to summarize the previous person's remarks aid in listening skills, or does it distract from the flow of the discussion?

What does your answer imply about the ways in which we are accustomed to listening?

Compare the last exercise with the previous two, in which this technique was not used. Which exercise inspired the best communication?

Exercise 20
FORMAL AND INFORMAL MEETINGS

Purpose: To help parents and staff understand the value of an informal setting to stimulate the flow of ideas and decisions.

Setting: A meeting of staff and/or parents in a room large enough to accommodate two sub-groups without noise interference; two sets of chairs (Set A in straight rows with a chairperson or leader seated in front; Set B arranged in a circle or around a table).

Time: Approximately one hour.

Materials: Pencils and paper for the chair persons.

INSTRUCTIONS

First, have everyone decide on a problem to solve during this exercise. The problem should be relevant to the group's current needs and agreed upon by a majority. Divide everyone into two sub-groups (Group A and Group B). Have each group choose a leader then distribute Instruction Sheets A and B to the respective groups. Once the discussions have begun, you may wish to check each group's progress, but do not interfere beyond this. [**30 minutes**]

After the allotted time, call the groups back together to discuss what has transpired in the problem-solving session. This process evaluation should include:

1. How each group functioned (similarities, differences).
2. Which group was more enjoyable to participate in.
3. Which group was more productive.
4. What was learned from this exercise and how it can be applied to the regular parent group meetings.

Notes to the Trainer: This exercise is especially helpful with parent and/or staff groups whose meetings tend to be formal and rigidly structured by parliamentary procedure. It provides an opportunity to experiment with alternative methods of group dynamics which will create less structure and more participation. While monitoring the progress of the groups, you should take notes for use in the later discussion.

In trying to solve the problem at hand, your group will function very formally. The chairperson must at all times enforce the rules of parliamentary procedure. In addition, the following rules must be observed:

1. Members should address each other only by their last names (Mr. Jones, Mrs. Smith, etc.).

2. No one may speak without first being recognized by the chairperson.

3. General discussion may not take place until there is a motion on the floor which has been seconded.

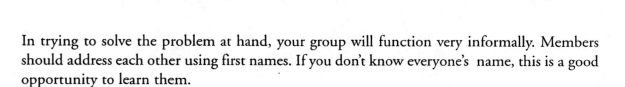

In trying to solve the problem at hand, your group will function very informally. Members should address each other using first names. If you don't know everyone's name, this is a good opportunity to learn them.

Go around the circle and introduce yourselves. (You might also want to tell the group one "good" thing about yourself: "I like myself because..." or "I do_____well" or "I think I'm a _____kind of person.")

The chairperson should encourage all group members to speak and should keep a record of decisions or suggestions made. He or she should set a "light" tone for the discussion.

Chapter 5
Group Planning and Organization

The purpose of this chapter is to refine the group planning and organizational skills begun in **Chapter 4**. The exercises included in **Chapter 5** have been chosen to help groups make the most effective use of their time, resources, and leadership talents, as well as to suggest ways of solving any problems that might arise as a result of the group dynamics.

This section also stresses the importance of a relaxed atmosphere to enhance productivity and the importance of accepting differing ideas and opinions of the group. Different styles of leadership are explored through the use of games and role-playing activities. An organized group is a productive group; one that leads to successful child development centers, schools, and, most importantly, to successful children.

> An "**assumption**" is: 1. a fact or statement taken for granted.
> 2. the supposition that something is true.

Exercise 21
GROUP PLANNING

> **Purpose:** To help parents become aware of the group's perceptions of what constitutes successful children.
>
> **Setting:** A room for any size group of parents.
>
> **Time:** Approximately two hours.
>
> **Materials:** Newsprint, magic markers, copies of *Worksheet 19: A Sample Plan and The Planning Process* and pencils for each participant.

INSTRUCTIONS

Explain the purpose and the reasons for conducting this exercise and the importance of mastering the art of planning in terms of productivity. You might offer some of the following reasons:

1. The group will have a clearly-defined goal, and therefore will be able to focus its energy.
2. It will have deadlines and times for doing certain tasks.
3. It will have tasks assigned to specific people who will bear responsibility for getting them done.
4. It will have a way of measuring its accomplishments.

Provide the definition of "planning" and thoroughly explain its process as outlined below. You might want to distribute the *Worksheet 19*, which uses the examples given in the sample lecture below, for further explanation.

Planning: Planning is simply deciding in advance what one is going to do at some point in the future. Since the future is not completely predictable, a potentially effective plan must be flexible enough to allow for changes to be made.

The Planning Process: There are four major parts to a good plan: the goal, the objectives, the course of action, and the evaluation. Each of these can be determined by asking specific questions:

(continued)

(continued from page 67)

1. **The Goal:** "What is to be accomplished?" Answer the question as simply as possible and in such a way that the group can later measure whether or not the goal was achieved. For example

   Goal A: Get more parents to come out to parent meetings.

   Goal B: Have thirty-five parents at next month's parent group meeting.

   Goal B is more clearly stated. It will therefore be easier for a group to determine whether or not it was achieved.

2. **The Objectives:** "How is the task to be accomplished?" If we continue to use **Goal B** as an example, the objectives stating how this is to be accomplished might be:

   A. Send notices home with children.

   B. Visit parents who have not been attending meetings.

   C. Telephone all parents to remind them of the meeting.

3. **The Course of Action:** "Who is to accomplish the objectives?" and "When are they to be accomplished?" Assign individuals specific responsibilities with deadlines to meet. To meet **Objective A**, the course of action might be:

   1. Mrs. Smith will write the notice by next Friday.

   2. Mr. Kennedy will make the copies of the notice within a week.

   3. Mrs. Allen, the teacher, will send the notices home with the children one week before the meeting.

Answer any questions about this sample plan and distribute pencils and copies of *Worksheet 14: A Sample Plan and the Planning Process* to each participant. Have the group define a goal and use the worksheets to develop a plan for accomplishing that goal. Emphasize that this should be an actual plan to be carried out, not just a "practice" one. **[15 minutes]**

After the allotted time, ask group members to come together and contribute their ideas for a "master" plan. Record the ideas on the newsprint. This method allows everyone to have an input in designing the master plan. As a trainer, your role is to assist the members, to to dictate the meeting.

After the plan has been completed, lead a group evaluation of the effectiveness and discuss other group activities that may be improved by similar planning techniques. The evaluation might also include an assessment of group process: who did/did not contribute to the discussion and why, etc. See "Process Evaluation" in the **Glossary**.

Notes to the Trainer: After this exercise, the group may be ready to design an overall plan for the year's activities. This meeting may be followed by subsequent training sessions to evaluate and, if necessary, redesign the original plan as the group's planning skills improve.

Worksheet 19
A SAMPLE PLAN AND THE PLANNING PROCESS

INSTRUCTIONS
Define a goal and use this worksheet to develop a plan for accomplishing the goal.

Goal (What?):

_____

_____

_____

_____

Objectives (How?)

_____

_____

_____

_____

Plan (Who? When?)

_____

_____

_____

_____

ILLUSTRATION OF FLOW CHART
The Planning Process

Goal (What is to be accomplished?)

    1. 35 parents at each meeting

Objective (How it is to be accomplished?)

    1. Send notices home

    2. Visit parents

    3. Telephone parents

(continued)

(continued from page 69)

Plan (Who will accomplish it? When will they accomplish it?)

1. Smith, Friday

2. Kennedy, Friday week

3. Allen, week from Friday

Evaluation (What happened at the meeting? Suggestions for improvements?)

1. 20 parents attended the meeting

2. Develop a "phone tree" to call and inform parents of future meetings

Exercise 22
EXPLORING GROUP INTERACTION

> **Purpose:** To assess the similarities and differences in the goals and values of staff and parent groups. Also to enable the groups to become aware of their decision-making processes and the existing leadership within the group.
>
> **Setting:** A meeting room for staff and parents to work in two separate groups, one of staff and one of parents, for the first portion of the exercise. They will be reassembled for the discussion at the conclusion of the exercise.
>
> **Time:** Approximately one hour.
>
> **Materials:** *Worksheet 20: Functions of a Child Development Program* rating sheet and pencils for each participant.

INSTRUCTIONS
Have everyone fill out the rating sheets individually.
[10 minutes]

When finished, form two groups, one of staff and one of parents and have everyone compare answers and reach a consensus. Tell the groups: "DO NOT choose a leader." **[25 minutes]**

Combine the two groups to discuss the following points:
1. Did you reach a consensus by logical reasoning, or did arguing occur?
2. Did you give in to appease the others and avoid conflict, or did you up stand for what you felt was right?
3. Did you employ conflict-reducing techniques (voting, bargaining, etc.) to reach decisions?
4. Did you feel that the original disagreements helped or hindered the decision-making processes?
5. Did you notice some people participating more than others?
6. Did you notice any particular person taking charge even though you were instructed not to choose a leader?
7. Did group members seem to lose interest when the discussion did not focus on them?

(continued)

(continued from page 71)

8. Did anyone become excited, angry, irritated, or discouraged?
9. Did any group member seem to get "stuck" on a particular idea and hold to it stubbornly, hindering the flow of the discussion? Was anyone confronted with the fact that he or she was doing this?
10. How do the priorities of the two groups (staff and parents) compare?

RATING SHEET

INSTRUCTIONS

Rank the following according to your opinion of their importance, "1" being the most important, then "2", and so on. You may add other functions to the list. [**10 minutes**]

____ A.. Child development programs should help children develop social maturity.

____ B. Child development programs should enrich home life for both the child and his or her family.

____ C. A child development program should be a place where parents develop contacts for employment and other community resources.

____ D. A child development program should keep its children warm, dry and well-fed while they are in attendance there.

____ E. A child development program should give a child a sense of security by providing a familiar environment, a "home-away-from-home."

____ F. A child development program should be an "experiment in living" for children in which they learn to interact with their peers.

____ G. Participation in parent activities should provide training for leadership in community work.

____ H. Parents and teachers should support and enhance the learning experiences of children.

____ I. A child development program should provide a child-centered environment, with adequate time for free play and self-expression.

____ J. A child development program should serve as a laboratory for democratic action.

(continued from page 73)

___ K. A child development program should provide social service support to families.

___ L. Parents should be involved with teachers in developing an individual educational plan for their children.

___ M. ....

___ N. ....

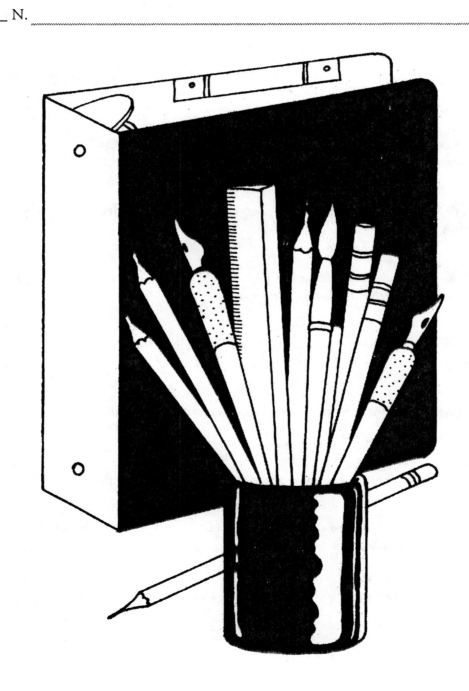

Exercise 23
PARENTS, TEACHERS AND PROBLEMS

Purpose: To acquaint the parent group with the differences within the group and to develop understanding of ways to relate to the group.

Setting: A room to accommodate any size group of parents.

Time: Approximately two hours.

Materials: Newsprint, magic markers, copies of *Worksheet 21: Self Assessment,* and pencils for each participant.

INSTRUCTIONS

Explain the purpose of the exercise and discuss the ways that different personalities can compliment each other and strengthen the total group, possibly using a newsprint sheet with the steps listed on it as a reference.

INSTRUCTIONS

The following questionnaire is intended to help you understand yourself and your reactions to other people. Read the questions carefully and answer "YES" or "NO."

1. Do you think that most problems begin because someone feels insecure, worthless and/or threatened?   YES   NO

2. If you feel threatened by someone, do you ever notice yourself trying to hurt the other person to protect yourself?   YES   NO

3. Do you ever notice yourself backing another person into a corner during an argument?   YES   NO

4. Do you ever put yourself in the other person's shoes to see and feel things as the other person sees and feels?   YES   NO

5. Do you ever find yourself giving in to anger and ridicule when someone disagrees with your opinions or suggestions?   YES   NO

6. Do you find that when you are tired and/or not feeling well that problems multiply and seem harder to cope with?   YES   NO

7. Do you want to work for things yourself rather than having them handed to you?   YES   NO

8. Do you believe that the best decision is one you make for yourself?   YES   NO

9. Do you generally recognize and accept other people as they are?   YES   NO

10. Are you willing to talk with and be seen with someone who is different from you?   YES   NO

11. Do you accept other people's differences?   YES   NO

(continued)

(continued from page 76)

12. Do you ever notice that sometimes what is not said is more important than what is said?

              YES   NO

13. Have you ever wanted to do something that you thought was right and then had someone else put doubts in your mind?

              YES   NO

14. Do you think that creating a better world requires participation on your part?

              YES   NO

15. Do you consider yourself to be an open-minded person?   YES   NO

16. Do you consider yourself to be a mature person?   YES   NO

Exercise 24
LEADERSHIP EXERCISE

Purpose: To understand differences in style and efficiency of leadership in parent groups.

Setting: A meeting of parents and/or staff in a room large enough to accommodate three "discussion groups" without noise interference.

Time: Approximately one and a half hours.

Materials: Newsprint, magic markers, copies of *Worksheet 22: Handout A, A Case Study* for each participant, and three copies of *Worksheet 23: Handout B, Role Instructions for Group Leaders.*

Purpose: To help group members evaluate factors that encourage or discourage volunteering.

Setting: A room for any size group of parents and/or teachers.

Time: Approximately one hour.

Materials: Newsprint, a magic marker, and 4-5 chairs facing the group in front of the room.

INSTRUCTIONS

Select three people as group leaders for the "discussion group" portion of the exercise, and allow them time to read through *Handout B*. Assign each leader a leadership style to role-play during the exercise. Stress the importance of staying in character during this exercise. As the leaders are preparing for their roles, have the rest of the group read *Handout A*.

Explain to the participants that the purpose of this exercise is to examine some of the different ways in which groups function. Inform them that group mem-

(continued)

(continued from page 78)

bers have been selected to lead three discussion groups, each using a different style of leadership. The following are the objectives of each group:

1. To develop a solution to the case study described in *Handout A*.
2. To observe and analyze the leadership style used by their group leader as they work to solve the problem.

Emphasize that there are no "right" or "wrong" solutions to the problems, and encourage a comfortable atmosphere. [**45 minutes**]

Monitor each group's progress without interfering, making notes for use in a later discussion. At the end of the allotted time, bring the three groups together and have the group leaders write their groups' suggested solutions on newsprint in front of the room. For the best comparison, have the "Democratic" group present last.

After hearing the reports (content of the group interaction), ask for comments from group members on the process, or functioning of the groups, especially on the behavior of the group leaders. You should also ask the leaders to describe how they felt in their roles (comfortable, uncomfortable, unsure of themselves, etc.). These comments should be listed on the newsprint next to the solutions proposed for each group. [**10 minutes**]

Then, aid the participants in evaluating the productivity of the three groups. Some suggestions for the discussion might be:

1. What was the relationship between the leadership style and the work accomplished (productivity)?
2. How did the group's feelings about the leader affect the group's productivity?
3. How did the leadership style affect the group's interaction?
4. Which group found its task most enjoyable?
5. Would the different styles of leadership be more appropriate in different situations?

[**15 minutes**]

Notes to the Trainer: This should be a "fun" exercise for everyone. It will work best if the leaders are effective in their roles. Be supportive to the leaders and remind the group that these leaders are playing roles *assigned* to them.

Worksheet 22—Handout A: A Case Study
LEADERSHIP EXERCISE

INSTRUCTIONS

Read the following case study and be prepared to discuss possible solutions to the problem.

The Leatherwood Parents Association is a newly-formed group of parents at Leatherwood Elementary School. Arthur Dennis, a teacher's aide, has spent two months contacting parents and developing informal discussion groups before a formal meeting. The group has met three times so far, once a week. At the first meeting, a parent, Mr. Warren, complained very vocally about the city schools and raised a number of issues which interested the rest of the group. In the first thirty minutes of the meeting, he was elected "Temporary Chairman." As the meeting progressed, it became clear that Mr. Warren was completely dominating the meeting and not allowing the other members to speak.

At the second meeting, attendance was down to about half that of the previous meeting. Again, Mr. Warren acted in a very authoritarian manner.

Arthur Dennis made follow-up contacts to those parents who did not attend the second meeting. When he asked them why they had not returned, they gave vague and unconvincing reasons.

The third meeting was held last night. Only five people showed up, and it was clear that no one was interested, including Mr. Warren, who made references to dropping out of the group. Nothing was accomplished and the meeting was postponed until next week.

Arthur is more than a little discouraged and doesn't know what to do next. Your group's task is to outline a plan by which he can rebuild a strong, cohesive group. Your leader should mediate the discussion.

Worksheet 23—Handout B: Role-Play Instructions
LEADERSHIP EXERCISE FOR GROUP LEADERS

INSTRUCTIONS

Familiarize yourself with the following leadership styles. Be prepared to play the leadership part assigned to you by the trainer. Remember, you must stay in character during the discussion.

GROUP LEADER NO. 1: AUTHORITARIAN

You make all decisions in your group and control all interactions. This can be done in either a forceful "drill sergeant" manner, or a paternalistic manner. In either case, you need to be in total control of the group.

GROUP LEADER NO. 2: LAISSEZ-FAIRE

The opposite of authoritarian. Exert no overt leadership, do not initiate any interaction, and respond only when questioned directly. Play a "hands off" role.

GROUP LEADER NO. 3: DEMOCRATIC

Function as a "helper" or "enabler" to the group. Encourage participation, summarize the discussion occasionally, and generally assist the group to make its own decisions.

Exercise 25
GROUP EVALUATION

Purpose: To help a group examine different ways of interaction among members and become aware of difficulties which may be blocking progress.

Setting: A meeting room for staff and/or parents, preferably of not more than fifteen members.

Time: Approximately 30 minutes.

Materials: Newsprint sheet with *Worksheet 24: Group Evaluation* duplicated on it, copies of the worksheet, and pencils for each participant.

INSTRUCTIONS

Explain the purpose of the exercise to the group and distribute the worksheets and pencils. Instruct the group to read through the questions first, then go back and circle the responses which best describe the last meeting the group had. When this task has been completed, the trainer should:

1. Lead the group in sharing and comparing their answers.
2. Record the most popular responses on the newsprint worksheet.
3. Lead the group in an evaluation of their responses. For example, what is the group doing "right"? What factors are contributing to this? Which factors undermine the group's effectiveness? What can be done to strengthen the group?

Note to the Trainer: This evaluation may be used at regular intervals to measure a group's progress.

Worksheet 24
GROUP EVALUATION

INSTRUCTIONS
Answer the following based on your group's last meeting.

1. Group Member Participation in the Discussion:

     a. no one dominated

     b. few people dominated

     c. several people did most of the talking

     d. everyone, or nearly everyone, participated

2. Success of Group Decision-Making:

     a. unable to reach any important decisions

     b. a few important decisions were reached

     c. several decisions of minor importance were reached

     d. several decisions of major importance were reached

3. Process Used in Group Decision-Making:

     a. no particular process

     b. bargaining or "trading"

     c. majority vote

     d. consensus

4. Clarity of Group Goals:

     a. unclear to everyone

     b. unclear to most members

     c. unclear to some members

     d. clear to most members

(continued)

(continued from page 83)

5. Group Atmosphere:

      a. discomfort

      b. tension

      c. openness

      d. comfort and cooperation

6. Group Listening:

      a. most did not listen carefully

      b. some listened carefully

      c. most listened somewhat carefully

      d. all listened carefully

7. Group Togetherness:

      a. very fragmented and discordant

      b. some lack of agreement

      c. most work well together

      d. harmonious

8. Group efficiency:

      a. inefficient

      b. sometimes efficient

      c. usually efficient

      d. always efficient

Exercise 26
QUICK STRESS REDUCING EXERCISES

> **Purpose:** To simulate a stressful situation in a group to explore and resolve tension, anxiety and conflict.
>
> **Setting:** Room for a small-to-medium size group.
>
> **Time:** Approximately one hour.
>
> **Materials:** None required.

INSTRUCTIONS

Follow the instructions for each exercise.

Exercise 1. Participants must silently form a line in which they position themselves in the order of their influence in the group. (Include the trainer.) [**15 minutes**]

Exercise 2. Each participant must choose father, mother, brother and sister figures from among the other group members. [**15 minutes**]

Exercise 3. Each participant must choose one person to be eliminated from the group. [**15 minutes**]

Notes to the Trainer: After each exercise is completed, have the group discuss the interaction that took place. Here are a few guides for discussion:
1. Was there laughter during the exercise? If so, was it because the situation was humorous, or because the participants were embarrassed, nervous, etc.?
2. What took place on a non-verbal level during the exercise (particularly *Exercise 1*)?
3. Did participants find the exercise uncomfortable?
4. Were some members hesitant about participating? Why?
5. In *Exercise 2*, did some people seem to get chosen repeatedly for a particular role? Why?
6. In *Exercise 3*, did the new group of "eliminated" people have anything in common?

Worksheet 25—Part A: Differing Values
VALUE CLARIFICATION

Purpose: To enable participants to recognize, value and utilize their differences in a positive way.

Setting: A room to accommodate any size group of parents and/or staff.

Time: Approximately one hour.

Materials: 5"x 8" index cards and pencils for the group members.

INSTRUCTIONS

Give a brief explanation of the purpose of this exercise, emphasizing the importance of appreciating differences, as well as, similarities among people. Distribute the cards and pencils to the participants and give them the following instructions: [**20 minutes**]

1. In the center of the card, write your name.

2. In the upper left-hand corner describe an occasion when you were valued for a unique characteristic as a staff member or parent.

3. In the upper right-hand corner, indicate your own unique traits that can be utilized by this group.

4. In the lower left-hand corner, describe an occasion when you recognized/valued/utilized another parent's or staff member's unique traits.

5. In the lower right-hand corner, list any fears you have about confrontations with others regarding your differences.

After this is done, ask the participants to find a partner by examining each other's cards until they find someone with an identified difference (upper right-hand corner of the cards) that they can accept, value and utilize. Ask the groups to form two concentric circles, one member of each pair taking a position in the inner circle and the other member taking a position in the outer circle. The inner circle group should share, compare and get to know each others differences, and then try to determine ways these differences can be utilized by the program. The outer circle group should assume the role of observers and consultants to those in the inner circle. [**20 minutes**]

Stop the process when the participants appear to have completed this task. Then, have the partners switch roles, moving from the inner circle to the outer circle and vice versa, to repeat the process. [**20 minutes**]

Purpose: To enable group members to analyze their time management.

Setting: A room for any size group of parents and/or staff.

Time: Approximately one hour.

Materials: 5"x 8" index cards and pencils for the group members.

INSTRUCTIONS

Explain the purpose of the exercise and distribute the pencils and cards to the group. Give the group the following instructions:

1. In the center of the card, write your name.

2. In the upper left-hand corner, list the activities in which you feel obligated to participate.

3. In the upper right-hand corner, list the activities which you feel are most important to you.

4. In the lower left-hand corner, list the activities which you feel are most important to people close to you (family, boss, etc.).

5. In the lower right-hand corner, list the activities that give you the most satisfaction.

[20 minutes]

Then, ask the participants to rank their activities in order of the amount of time spent on each, placing a "1" next to the activity which takes up most of their time, etc. Have the participants form into sub-groups of three or four to discuss the implications of the ranking. **[20 minutes]** You may want to offer some of the following suggestions for discussion topics:

Do we value the demands of others over our own desires?

Do we spend time on activities which give us the most satisfaction?

Do we consider activities important because they give us satisfaction, or must they produce other, more visible results?

Do we tend to under-rate the importance of enjoyable activities?

(continued)

(continued from page 87)

You may want to bring the participants together to share their conclusions with everyone. Use the following questions to focus the discussion:

How do we pass these attitudes on to our children or students?

Is there evidence of such attitudes in the child development program's curriculum?

Should this situation be changed, and if so, how?

[20 minutes]

Exercise 27
TRYING OUT OPPOSITE STYLES

Purpose: Examine different ways group members interact during meetings and to become aware of any difficulties which may be blocking group progress.

Setting: A meeting room for staff and/or parents (maximum 15 members).

Time: Approximately one hour.

Materials: Newsprint, copies of *Worksheet 27: Opposites* and pencils for each participant.

INSTRUCTIONS

Explain the purpose of the exercise to the group and distribute the *Worksheet 27: Opposites* and pencils.

Worksheet 27
OPPOSITES

INSTRUCTIONS

This exercise is designed to give you insight into perspectives other than your own. For each given pair of personalities, pick the one that is most opposite to yours and try out that style during the meeting. After the exercise, write any notes or reactions that you had during the meeting.

If you are:

A Planner/Spontaneous—If you are a careful planner, try being as spontaneous as possible, and vice versa.

An Approval Seeker/An Initiator—If you are always waiting for a consensus before you act, try being the initiator, and vice versa.

A Helper/Self-Centered—If you are always trying catering to other people's needs, try focusing on meeting your personal needs, and vice versa.

Rational/Imaginative—If you are very rational and a "systematic" thinker, then try to be more imaginative in expressing yourself, and vice versa

A Listener of Words/Listener of Feelings—If you are in the habit of listening only to "words", try to focus on what people are "saying", and vice versa.

A Leader/A Follower—If you always lead the discussion/meeting, then follow someone else's lead, and vice versa.

Notes and Reactions:

....

....

....

....

....

Exercise 28
WIN AS MUCH AS YOU CAN

Purpose: To enable group members to understand conflict, competition and cooperation.

Setting: A room for four groups to work comfortably.

Time: Approximately an hour and a half.

Materials: *Worksheet 28: Win as Much as You Can* tally sheet.

INSTRUCTIONS

Divide everyone into four separate groups (of two or more people per group) and distribute *Worksheet 28* to each group. If you have a large group you can have the participants choose a partner.

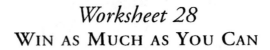

INSTRUCTIONS

For ten successive rounds you and your partner will choose either an X or a Y. Each round's payoff depends on the pattern of choices made in your cluster.

PAYOFF SCHEDULE

4 X's:	LOSE $1.00 EACH
3 X's:	WIN $1.00 EACH
1 Y:	LOSE $3.00 EACH
2 X's:	WIN $2.00 EACH
2 Y's:	LOSE $2.00 EACH
1 X:	WIN $3.00 EACH
3 Y's:	LOSE $1.00 EACH
4 Y's:	WIN $1.00 EACH

You are to confer with your partner in each round and make a *joint decision*. In rounds 5, 8, and 10 you and your partner may first confer with the other dyads in your cluster before making your joint decision, as before.

SCORECARD

	ROUND	YOUR CHOICE (CIRCLE)	CLUSTER'S PATTERN OF CHOICES	PAYOFF	BALANCE
	1	X Y	__ X __ Y		
	2	X Y	__ X __ Y		
	3	X Y	__ X __ Y		
	4	X Y	__ X __ Y		
Bonus Round: (payoff x 3)	5	X Y	__ X __ Y		
	6	X Y	__ X __ Y		
	7	X Y	__ X __ Y		
Bonus Round: (payoff x 8)	8	X Y	__ X __ Y		
	9	X Y	__ X __ Y		
Bonus Round: (payoff x 10)	10	X Y	__ X __ Y		

92   (continued)

(continued from page 92)

WIN AS MUCH AS YOU CAN
REACTION SHEET

1. How do I feel about myself in this exercise:

2. How do I feel about my partner's influence:

3. How do I feel about the others in my group:

4. What I have learned from this exercise:

Chapter 6
Working Together to Develop the Program

The purpose of this chapter is to provide practical experience in the major policy and decision making tasks in your program.

The success of the exercises in this section will depend greatly on how well your group has mastered the techniques in **Chapters 3** and **4**. If your group members are having difficulty with these exercises, consider conducting additional exercises from one or both of the two preceding chapters. In particular, *Exercise 24: Group Evaluation* should be helpful in assisting you and your group to pinpoint the source of any problems.

As with the previous two chapters, the trainer may wish to refer to the data from the diagnostic instruments in **Chapter 2** to help evaluate training needs in the areas of policy and decision-making and to select the appropriate training exercises.

Exercise 29
VOLUNTEERING

> **Purpose:** To help group members experience some of the feelings that encourage and discourage volunteering
>
> **Setting:** A group of parents and staff, any size.
>
> **Time:** Approximately one hour.
>
> **Materials:** Newsprint, a magic markers, and a group of chairs set aside or to the front of the main group.

INSTRUCTIONS

Announce to the group that volunteers will be needed for an experiment. Ask those who would like to volunteer to raise their hands. Pick the volunteers and ask them to sit in the chairs facing the main group. Once they are seated, announce to the group that the experiment is over, and with the volunteers remaining where they are, lead a discussion,
focusing on the following points: [**15 minutes**]

1. What feelings were people experiencing as they contemplated whether or not to volunteer? (Give the group a few moments to recall their feelings).
2. What factors influenced their decision? (the way the problem was stated, the reaction of the other group members, etc.). Draw out responses from those who volunteered as well as those who did not. You may also ask the volunteers to share their feelings with each other, then report to the larger group.

Make two lists on the newsprint using the reactions given by the participants: [**10 minutes**]
1. Factors that encourage volunteering (the encouragement of others, the desire to participate or be helpful, curiosity, group pressure, etc.)
2. Factors that discourage volunteering (uncertainty of the situation, lack of confidence, group size, waiting for others, etc.)

Lead the group in a discussion of these factors and their effects on the level of parent involvement. Focus on specific ways to encourage volunteering and parent involvement. [**10 minutes**]

Exercise 30
DEVELOPING THE EDUCATIONAL PROGRAM
Part A: Setting Goals

Purpose: To assist parents and staff in developing goals for the program based upon the educational needs of the children.

Setting: A meeting of staff and parents, any size.

Time: Approximately two hours.

Materials: Newsprint, magic markers, and copies of *Worksheet 29, Goals for the Child Development Program,* for each participant.

INSTRUCTIONS

Explain that this is a two-part exercise in curriculum and activity development. The first step will be to decide on the program's goals. Based on the educational and developmental needs of the children. Refer to the previous exercise, reviewing the definitions that were established for "goal" and "objectives." The goals are WHAT the program is intended to accomplish. The objectives are HOW these goals will be met. Divide the participants into two sub-groups of parents and staff, and distribute copies of *Worksheet 29: Goals and Objectives for the Child Development Program*, pencils and paper to each participant. Have each individual read over the handout and use it as a guide to develop his/her own list. [**20 minutes**]

Then have everyone discuss and compare answers in their groups and compile one list for the group. [**20 minutes**]

Reassemble the two groups and lead them in a discussion of their ideas, focusing on common points between the groups. The goals which are understood and agreed upon by the entire group should be recorded on newsprint. Ample time should be allowed for this portion of the exercise. The process of thinking carefully through alternative goals and becoming acquainted with the views of fellow-parents may be even more important to the growth of the educational program than the final list. [**40 minutes**]

Finally, have the goals ranked in the order of importance either by consensus or majority vote. Allow time for thorough discussion of each item. The trainer may duplicate and/or have copies mailed out prior to the following session. [**10 minutes**]

(continued)

(continued from page 96)

Notes to the Trainer: A group should meet the following criteria before conducting this exercise:

1. A full representation of parents and teachers involved in the child development program.
2. Prior experience sharing and planning activities together such as the *X-Ray of the Parent/Teacher* exercise.

Set aside time to discuss goals that may be appropriate at each parent group meeting. At a minimum, the trainer should take a few minutes in subsequent meetings of the group to follow up on their progress.

This exercise is designed to prepare the group for the exercise immediately following: *Developing the Educational Program, Part B: Curriculum for the Child Development Program*, which provides an opportunity for the group to apply its stated goals to the day-to-day program of the school or child development center.

Worksheet 29
GOALS FOR THE CHILD DEVELOPMENT PROGRAM

INSTRUCTIONS

This is a guide to developing your own list of goals and objectives for your program. List as many specific objectives as possible for the goals given. Then, list additional goals and objectives in the blank spaces provided.

GOAL: Maintaining the child's good health

OBJECTIVES: a. Institute a diet and exercise program.

        b. _____

        c. _____

GOAL: Helping the child's emotional and social development

OBJECTIVES: a. Train teachers to encourage self-expression and self-discipline.

        b. _____

        c. _____

GOAL: Improving the child's ability to think and speak clearly

OBJECTIVES: a. Insure contact between child and adults and/or older children.

        b. _____

        c. _____

GOAL: Improving the child's understanding of the world he or she lives in.

OBJECTIVES: a. Include a wide range of experiences in the program.

        b. _____

        c. _____

GOAL: Helping the child build self-confidence, self-respect and dignity

OBJECTIVES: a. Arrange for activities that give the child frequent chances to succeed.

        b. _____

        c. _____

(continued)

(continued from page 98)

GOAL: Encouraging the child to want to learn.

OBJECTIVES: a. Train staff to foster a climate of reassurance and stimulation.

    b. _____

    c. _____

GOAL: Strengthening the child's family ties.

OBJECTIVES: a. Institute an effective parent involvement program which will increase the parents' understanding of the child's educational experience.

    b. _____

    c. _____

GOAL: Developing in the child a responsible attitude toward society.

OBJECTIVES: a. Ensure children's involvement in community activities.

    b. _____

    c. _____

GOAL: _____

OBJECTIVES: a. _____

    b. _____

    c. _____

GOAL: _____

OBJECTIVES: a. _____

    b. _____

    c. _____

GOAL: _____

OBJECTIVES: a. _____

    b. _____

    c. _____

Exercise 31
DEVELOPING THE EDUCATIONAL PROGRAM
Part B: Curriculum for the Child Development Program

Purpose: To assist a group of parents and staff in working together to develop the program's curriculum, based on the goals set in Part A of this exercise.

Setting: A meeting of staff and parents in a room large enough to accommodate several "discussion groups" without noise interference.

Time: Approximately two hours.

Materials: Newsprint, magic markers, and copies of the final list of goals set by the group in the previous session.

INSTRUCTIONS

Begin by reviewing the goals that were set for the program in the previous session. Explain that the purpose of this session is to determine methods of implementing these goals. You should suggest that the participants focus on two areas:

a. Types of activities that will be needed.

b. Materials and equipment needed to carry out these activities.

Form small discussion groups of 4-5, containing both parents and staff. Assign different goals from Part A for each group to use to discuss:

1. If and how the goal is being realized in the child development program.

2. Ideas for new ways to realize this goal.

[**30 minutes**]

After the discussion, regroup everyone together and have a representative from each group present the ideas discussed. [**30 minutes**]

Open the floor up for a question/answer session in which members are allowed free exchange with one another to clarify ideas. Oversee the dialogue and write down major points discussed on newsprint in front of the room. After this exchange, you may turn the session over to the parent group leader of chairperson for a discussion. [**60 minutes**]

(continued)

(continued from page 100)

Notes to the Trainer: This is a complex training exercise, but it can be very rewarding for the parents as they have input in the plans for their children's education. Preparation for this exercise should include having parents review the list of goals at home and think of suggestions for how to implement them. You might also want to give them some additional resource to look over at home before this session.

The success of this exercise depends on the ability of a group of parents and staff to exchange knowledge and ideas freely with each other. The group should have mastered the techniques presented in **Chapter 5** before attempting this exercise. If you feel confident that your group members are capable of working together productively on their own, just monitor the progress of the discussion and refrain from interfering. You may want to take notes for use in the later discussion.

Clearly, developing a curriculum for a child development program is not a task to be completed in one meeting. This training exercise should serve as a model for a group to use repeatedly during regular meetings to set its own goals and develop a program based on these goals.

Exercise 32
STAFF HIRING

Purpose: To acquaint the parent group with the basic procedures of recruiting, screening, and hiring staff.

Setting: A room for any size group of parents.

Time: Approximately two hours.

Materials: Newsprint, magic markers, copies of *Worksheet 30: Hiring Data Sheet* and *Worksheet 31: Basic Information Sheet, Employment Application* handouts, and pencils for each participant.

INSTRUCTIONS

The trainer should explain the purpose of the exercise and go over the following steps in hiring personnel, using newsprint with the steps listed on it as a reference:

1. Review job specifications.
2. Recruit applicants.
3. Screen applicants through the use of:
    a. application forms
    b. references
    c. personal interviews
4. Select and hire person for position.

Explain that this exercise involves the use of two different techniques, brainstorming and role-playing. You might want to give a brief explanation of each of these techniques, consulting the **Glossary**.

Begin the first part of the exercise, which involves brainstorming, by distributing pencils and copies of the *Basic Information Sheet* to the participants. Explain to the participants that they will need to become familiar with the information on the sheet before they can begin the hiring process. In the case of your particular program, these requirements may be set forth in the school by-laws, the program proposal, etc., or they may be determined at the discretion of a personnel committee. You may wish to rewrite the *Basic Information*

(continued)

(continued from page 102)

Sheet to conform to the requirements of your specific program. [**20 minutes**]

You should give the group a few minutes to look over the sheet, asking everyone to consider the information in terms of the question, "How would I recruit applicants for such a job opening?" (The process of informing as many potentially qualified people as possible about the opening in order to find the best possible person for the job is known as "recruitment.") Ask them to discuss their ideas while you record the suggestions on newsprint. Some suggestions might include: sending notices home with children, running articles in local newspapers, etc. [**10 minutes**]

After the brainstorming session, ask the group to suppose that three people have submitted applications for this position. Conduct a role-play exercise to simulate the hiring process. Nine volunteer actors will be needed for this: three "applicants," three "references," and three members of the personnel committee. The rest of the group will function as observers and should be instructed to record their observations on the reverse side of the Basic Information Sheet. When the volunteers have stepped to the front, you should distribute the Hiring Data Sheets to everyone except the personnel committee. Each member of the personnel committee should receive copies of all three Employment Applications. Each applicant and his or her respective "reference" should receive a copy of that applicant's Employment Application, as well as a Hiring Data Sheet. Allow a few minutes for the participants to review the handout(s). [**10 minutes**]

Instruct the personnel committee to convene privately and outline some of the questions they intend to ask the applicants and references. At the same time, the applicants should be instructed to consult with their references about what they intend to say in their interviews with the personnel committee. [**5 minutes**]

Next, the references should appear before the personnel committee, one at a time, to be interviewed. Remind the observers to take notes for later use. Each applicant should be interviewed for about ten minutes. When all of the interviews have been completed, instruct the personnel committee to confer for approximately ten minutes to evaluate the applicants and make a selection before announcing the decision to the group. [**10 minutes per interview**]

Lead a discussion focusing on the following points (making sure to give the actors a chance to respond before the observers make their comments):
What were the strong and weak points of the role-play?
How could it have been improved?

(continued)

(continued from page 103)

How well did the personnel committee function as a group?

Did they elicit information which enabled them to choose the best possible person for the job?

Did they seem to have a clear idea of what they were looking for?

[20 minutes]

Notes to the Trainer: Before conducting this exercise, you might want to review the rules of role- playing set forth in the **Glossary** and in **Chapter** 3, *Exercise 10.* Role-Play should, ideally, be enjoyable and non-threatening to the participants. It is important to be supportive and encouraging. This exercise offers a unique opportunity for the parents to find out what type of staff they would like to have for their program.

Worksheet 30
HIRING DATA SHEET

MRS. GRADY

Mrs. Grady is a teacher who lives in the community and is active in community affairs. She cares deeply for children, and the children in her class nearly always seem happy and relaxed and ready to learn. Her inability to keep files very well has been overlooked because of her excellence in working with children. She has a very low income, five children, and could definitely use the extra money that this position would provide.

MR. SHIPLEY

Mr. Shipley is a retired kindergarten teacher who lives in the suburbs. He has found retirement boring and would like to go back to work. As a kindergarten teacher, he was instrumental in introducing new methods of teaching, and his class was used as a model for the training of new teachers. His teaching experiences have been generally in middle-class schools.

MISS PETERS

Miss Peters has grown up in the community and has been involved in many community and environmental activities. She has just graduated from college and is anxious to return to the community and make a contribution. Miss Peters and her family are well known and respected in the community. She was able to get through college with some financial help from her parents and would not be considered a low-income person.

Worksheet 31
BASIC INFORMATION SHEET

Job Opening: Teacher

Salary: $22,000 per year

Reports To: Principal of the school

Duties:

      1. Primary responsibility for class of twenty children.

      2. Designs daily activity plans.

      3. Supervises teacher aides and volunteers.

      4. Makes home visits to parents to discuss the program.

      5. Maintains individual files on children.

Qualifications:

      1. Two years of college or equivalent experience (either volunteer or paid) in early childhood development.

      2. Knowledge of problems of low and middle income communities.

      3. Ability to relate and involve parents in the program.

Handout: Employment Application A

Name: Mrs. Kathleen (Katie) Grady

Age: 43

Address: 714 DeKalb Avenue

Marital Status: Separated

Family: Five children, ages 4-12

Education: Goodman Central High School, Graduated

Employment:

    1970-present: Teacher Aide, Head Start

    1964-1970: Waitress, Sally's Grill

    1959-1964: Domestic Work

Volunteer Experience:

    Church activities

    DeKalb Avenue Block Club

    Assistant Girl Scout Group Leader

    Head Start Volunteer

Handout: Employment Application B

Name: Mr. Jim Shipley

Age: 57

Address: 9264 Parkview Boulevard

Marital Status: Widower

Family: Two sons, 27 and 31

Education:

> Parkview High School, Graduated
>
> Central State Teachers College, B.A.
>
> North Central State University, M.Ed.
>
> (Early Childhood Education)

Employment:

> 1970-present, Retired
>
> 1957-1970, Kindergarten teacher,
>
> City Public Schools

Volunteer Experience:

> Amnesty International
>
> Community Watch Program
>
> NAACP

HANDOUT: EMPLOYMENT APPLICATION C

Name: Miss Alma Peters

Age: 23

Address: 619 9th Street

Marital Status: Single

Family: None

Education:

       Goodman Central High School, Graduated

       Calvin Coolidge Teachers College, B.A.

       (Early Childhood Education)

Employment:

       Part-time jobs during college

       Neighborhood Youth Corps, 3 months;

       Student Assistant, 6 months

Volunteer Experience:

       Volunteer at Local Recycling Center (college)

       St. James Tutoring Program

       Parkview Terrace Tenants Council

Chapter 7
Evaluating the Training

True success of our training can only be measured by the extent of parent involvement in the educational program. However, this information may not be available for some time after the training program. A complete evaluation requires detailed measuring instruments, to be administered periodically to keep up with changes in thinking and behavior. It is important for you to elicit reactions from the trainees as well as to evaluate the training from your own point of view. This can be done both informally, in conversations with the trainees, and during personal reflection following each training session. It will be easier to recall these reactions in the future when you make a comparison between sessions or an assessment of the overall program if these reactions are recorded properly.

The evaluation of training programs often receives low priority. When time is limited, evaluation is the first area of training to be eliminated. Sometimes you may simply forget to do an evaluation, or you may prefer to avoid candid comments from the participants after a particularly bad session. Overcoming these and other obstacles will result in effective evaluations and an increased quality of training.

The forms which follow have been designed to assist you in eliciting trainee reactions and in organizing your personal reflections. They serve a twofold purpose: they help the trainer measure the effect of the training, and they provide information to be used in planning future sessions. *Worksheet 32: Evaluation of Session by Trainee* should be completed by group participants immediately following a training session. When you instruct group members to complete this form, you should tell them that it is not necessary to sign their names to it, emphasizing that it is not an evaluation *of* them, but *by* them. If they know that the information will be used in designing future sessions, it will encourage them to respond to the questions candidly. You should fill out *Worksheet 33: Trainer Self-Evaluation* while the training session is still fresh in your mind.

The completed forms should be saved so that, as the training program proceeds, you can at least partially measure the progress of the group. These forms will not provide a final or precise measurement of training effectiveness; in other words, they will not determine whether you have done a "good" or "bad" job. What they will provide is some subjective information about sessions that may serve as a guide to what types of techniques and exercises are most effective with a particular group.

Exercise 32
GROUP EVALUATION

Purpose: To evaluate the effectiveness of the training session.

Setting: A room for small group.

Time: Approximately 15 minutes.

Materials: *Worksheet 32: Evaluation of Session by Trainee, Worksheet 33: Trainer Self Evaluation* and pencils.

INSTRUCTIONS

Ask each group member to fill out the evaluation handout (signing names is optional).

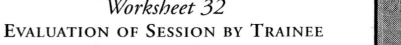

INSTRUCTIONS

Fill out the following evaluation. Be as honest and thorough as possible in your answers. Names are optional.

Group: _____ Date: _____

1. To what extent were the training objectives reached?

   a. fully

   b. partially

   c. not at all

2. In your judgment, describe the length of the workshop.

   a. about right

   b. too long

   c. too short

3. How would you classify the amount of time spent on lecturing and discussion? (You may respond more than once if necessary)

   a. too much/little/just enough lecture

   b. too much/little/just enough discussion

   c. about the right amount of each

4. Was enough time allowed for task completion and questions?   YES   NO

5. Did the workshop make you change your thinking or approach concerning the subjects discussed?

   a. none

   b. very little

   c. moderately so

   d. a lot

112   (continued)

(continued from page 112)

6. Would you recommend this workshop to others?

    a. YES (who?)

    b. NO (why not?)

7. How would you rate the workshop overall?

    a. poor

    b. fair

    c. good

    d. very good

    e. excellent

8. Circle any of the following statements that describe your feelings about this training session:

    a. It was exactly what I wanted.

    b. It was relevant to the group's concerns.

    c. I was mildly disappointed; it didn't hold my interest..

    d. It didn't deal with issues relevant to my group's concerns.

    e. It was a complete waste of time; I didn't learn anything.

9. Circle any of the following statements which apply to your training experience:

    a. The trainer allowed the group to make its own decisions.

    b. The trainer made certain that everyone had a chance to participate.

    c. The trainer was organized in presenting the material.

    d. The trainer accomplished the goals he or she had set for the sessions.

    e. The trainer set a relaxed and comfortable atmosphere.

    f. The trainer was focused on the group's concerns.

10. What were the strongest points of the session?

(continued)

(continued from page 113)

---

11. What were the weakest points of the session?

12. What did you learn during this session?

    a. new information:

    b. new skills:

13. Suggestions for future sessions:

Worksheet 33
TRAINER SELF-EVALUATION

INSTRUCTIONS

Fill out the following evaluation after each training session. When the information is fresh on your mind. Keep a file of the forms for future reference.

Group: .... Date: ....

1. Attendance:

   Parents: ....

   Staff: ....

   Others (visitors, administrators, etc.): ....

2. Objectives for this session:

....

....

....

3. Training design for achieving objectives:

....

....

....

4. Summary of what took place during the session (particularly deviations from training plans):

....

....

....

5. To what extent were objectives for the session accomplished?

....

....

....

(continued)   115

(continued from page 115)

6. What I did best in the session:

_____

_____

_____

7. What I could improve upon if I were to repeat this session:

_____

_____

_____

8. How would I rate the training overall?

_____

_____

_____

9. Follow-up planned with this group:

_____

_____

_____

10. Additional Comments:

_____

_____

_____

_____

_____

_____

_____

_____

Glossary

Brainstorming: A technique used to bring out new and creative ideas regarding a specific topic. The purpose is to produce a large number of ideas, even wildly impractical ones, which can then be narrowed down later. In many cases, an idea which initially seems impractical may lead to other, more practical ones. Participants are given a problem, idea, or situation, and are encouraged to think of as many solutions or related ideas as possible in a short period of time (usually 3—10 minutes). All suggestions are recorded, and an evaluation or processing of ideas is conducted to narrow down the list. The trainer may want to contribute a few ideas initially to get the discussion started.

Discussion Group or Sub-Group: A small group, sub-divided from a larger group for discussion purposes. A time limit is set for the discussion, after which the entire group reassembles to go over the topics covered. This technique sets an informal climate and encourages participation from those reluctant to speak out in a larger group. The discussion topics assigned should be specific and clear to all participants before the groups begin working. Examples of discussion group activities can be found in **Chapter 3**, *Exercise 4: Exploring Who I Am*, and *Exercise 9: Parent/Staff Participation*.

Climate Setting: Techniques used to set the training environment for maximum group interaction. For example, chairs placed in a circle or around a table encourage communication by letting all participants see one another and by eliminating the traditional leader or "authority figure," to facilitate equal exchange of ideas. Ice-breakers and other games that allow members to get to know one another help set a relaxed atmosphere. An example of these types of exercises can be found in **Chapter 3,** *Exercise 5: Exploring Who I Am* and *Exercise 10: Role-Play.*

Collaboration: A process in which group members work together to achieve a common goal. Leaders should not be assigned and everyone should function as equals in the decision-making process. An example of this technique can be found in **Chapter 5**, *Exercise 20: Exploring Group Interaction.*

Consensus: Universal agreement among group members. (*Note*: A consensus requires a unanimous decision. Voting is usually not used since more than a majority vote would be necessary. Naturally, consensus is more difficult to attain than a majority opinion, and various techniques may be employed to obtain a consensus (bargaining, negotiating, etc.).

Diagnosis: A process to determine concerns, resources, and effectiveness of the group. (See *Needs Assessment* for further definition.)

Facilitator: "Trainer." One who conducts the training session. The leader's focus should be on helping rather than on dictating the group.

Handout: Written materials which are distributed during an exercise. The trainer should review the contents of the handout with the group to clarify points and answer questions.

Intervention: An act intended to influence the feelings or behavior of a group. This can be an exercise, in which the group learns by experience, or a demonstration, like the showing of a film. The effectiveness of an intervention is measured by the corresponding change in the group's behavior.

Needs Assessment: A process used to determine the training needs of an individual, group, or organization. The first step is gathering information through interviews or questionnaires, followed by an evaluation of the training needs, to determine knowledge, skill, and efficacy of the group.

Objective: Training goals to be accomplished. The trainer and trainees should share common objectives for the training session.

Participatory or Interactive Training: Training techniques which permit both trainer and trainees to take active parts. Frequently used techniques of interactive training include brainstorming, discussion groups, and role-playing. Refer to the **Glossary** for detailed descriptions.

Process Evaluation: An examination of group interaction rather than the content of the matters being discussed. "Content" refers to the subject or the task at hand. Process, or dynamics, is concerned with the ways members work with one another. Factors such as morale, tone or atmosphere, participation, influence, leadership, conflict, competition, cooperation and many more are considered in a process evaluation. Process evaluation of group interaction is an effective way to diagnose and deal with group problems that often go unnoticed when the focus is primarily on the content. Most of the exercises in this book are intended to be followed by a process evaluation of some sort, in addition to an evaluation of the content.

Role-Playing: A technique in which two or more group members "act out" a problem or situation, followed by a discussion. Role-playing can be used to practice skills needed in real life situations. It can also provide an opportunity for the participants to see a situation from a different point of view. Role-playing exercises require group members to be relaxed and comfortable with each other; climate setting exercises may be helpful before a role-play. Specific instructions for role-playing are found in **Chapter 3**.

Simulation Training: Training in which situations are created or simulated to help participants learn a skill or concept. This technique provides vivid illustrations to clarify difficult concepts. One example of simulation training is role-playing. See **Chapter 6**, *Exercise 32: Staff Hiring*.

Suggested Resource Materials

Anderson, Phyllis. *Turning Our Schools Around: Seven Common Sense Steps to School Improvement*. Scherer Communications, 1995.

Collins, Marva and Civia Tamarkin. *Marva Collin's Way: Returning to Excellence in Education*. G.P. Putnam's Sons, 1990.

Comer, James P. *School Power: Implications of an Intervention Project*.

The Free Press, 1995.

Delpit, Lisa. *Other People's Children: Cultural Conflict in the Classroom*. The New Press, 1995.

Dodd, Anne Wescott. *A Parent's Guide to Innovative Education: Working with Teachers, Schools, and Your Children for Real Learning*. Noble Press, 1992.

Fiske, Edward B. *Smart Schools, Smart Kids: Why Do Some Schools Work?* Simon & Schuster, 1992.

Glasser, William, M.D. *Schools Without Failure*. Harper and Row, 1969.

Goodlad, John I. and Pamela Keating, ed. *Access to Knowledge: The Continuing Agenda for Our Nation's Schools, Revised Edition*. College Entrance Exam Board, 1994.

Hirsch, Jr., E.D. *The Schools We Need & Why We Don't Have Them*. Doubleday, 1996.

Martin, Jane Roland. *The Schoolhome: Rethinking Schools for Changing Families*. Harvard University Press, 1992.

Martz, Larry. *Making Schools Better: How Parents and Teachers Across the Country Are Taking Action--And How You Can, Too*. Times Books, 1992.

Morrison, Emily Kittle. *Leadership Skills: Developing Volunteers for Organizational Success*. Fisher Books, 1994

Oakes, Jeannie and Martin Lipton. *Making the Best Schools: A Handbook for Parents, Teachers, and Policymakers*. Yale University Press, 1990.

Reader Evaluation Form

INSTRUCTIONS

Your assistance in helping us evaluate this publication will be most valuable. Please fill out the form and mail it to the address provided below.

1. Does this book provide the kind of information that is helpful to you?   YES   NO

2. Does it contain information and advice which is new to you?   YES   NO

3. Is the book easy to read and understand?   YES   NO

4. Is the subject presented in an interesting style?   YES   NO

5. Does the book omit substantial information that you believe should be included?

YES   NO

6. Do your ideas about parent involvement conflict with the ideas presented in this book?

YES   NO

If yes, please share some of your ideas with us:

7. Name: (optional)

Title:

Location of Program:

MAIL TO
Humanics Publishing
PO Box 7400
Atlanta, GA 30357

Printed in the United States
17922LVS00001B/9-18

9 780893 341657